WILLIAMS-SONOMA

kids parties

Author	Lisa Atwood
Photography	Thayer Allyson Gowdy
Food Styling	Erin Quon
Styling	Bergren Rameson

Oxmoor House®

8

birthdays

*Party Themes, Favors,
Activities, and Games*

••

*Ideas for Decorating
Birthday Cakes,
Ice Cream Treats,
and Cookies*

82

halloween party

Blood-Red Punch

••

Caramel Apples

••

"Dirty" Popcorn Balls

••

Pumpkin Bread

cupcake party

*Vanilla Cupcakes with
Vanilla Frosting*

··

*Chocolate Cupcakes with
Chocolate Frosting*

36

easter party

Fresh-Squeezed Lemonade

··

Melon Ball Salad

··

Easter Egg Lollipops

··

*Garden-Top Carrot
Cupcakes with Cream
Cheese Frosting*

52

backyard party

Chex Mix

··

Corn on the Cobettes

··

*Fire-Roasted
Sausages on Sticks*

··

S'mores

68

tiki party

Fruit Smoothies

··

Lava Flows

··

Hawaiian Chicken Kebabs

··

Mango Dipping Sauce

96

pizza party

Pizza Dough

··

Quick Tomato Sauce

··

Chopped Green Salad

112

winter party

Hot Spiced Cider

··

Snugglers

··

Cheese Fondue

··

Chocolate Fondue

126

birthday recipes

Cakes

··

*Frostings, Glazes,
Icings, and Fillings*

··

Ice Creams and Sauces

··

Cookies

about this book

Throwing a fun and memorable party for kids can be easy and stress free when you're equipped with lots of good ideas and helpful hints. You'll find plenty of both in the following pages, including detailed work plans for getting party tasks done; dozens of kid-friendly recipes; ideas for crafts, games, and other party-time activities; and creative suggestions for invitations and decorations.

Whether you're celebrating a birthday, a holiday, or just the fun of being together, this book will help you plan the occasion. If it's summertime and you're thinking about hosting an outdoor party, look for the tips on hosting a cookout and organizing lawn games and relay races. Or, maybe it's wintertime and hot apple cider, fondue, and a snowflake-making contest sound good. They're here, too. You'll also find suggestions for cupcake and cookie decorating, pizza making, and lots more. The recipes combine what kids like to eat with easy-to-follow instructions parents appreciate, and all of them can be adapted to suit personal tastes and party themes. The result? You'll enjoy the party as much as the kids will.

birthdays

Most kids anticipate their special day all year long. Making it a blast is a snap with a few creative ideas and some tips for seeing them through. And it's easy to customize everything, from the cake to the fun to the favors, for your special child.

The first step towards making any celebration a rousing success is to consider the personality and temperament of the birthday boy or girl, then tailor the day to suit the honoree. Whether your child is an athlete or an artist, an angler or a budding scientist, there's a party theme to match every age and interest. With a little ingenuity, you can make any favorite activity, hobby, or pastime the basis of a birthday party.

fun food Plan the menu with the celebrant, the theme, and a bit of caprice in mind. If pizza is king, have kids decorate their own, creating faces with cut vegetables. If sandwiches are a favorite, cut them into playful shapes. Think cookouts, made-to-order treats, gooey fondues for dipping. Focusing on unexpected kid-friendly dishes will help make the occasion special.

party décor A few fanciful decorations can go a long way toward making your party memorable. Colorful helium-filled balloons and gauzy paper streamers give a celebratory tone to any setting, but more creative and personalized touches can make your occasion truly unforgettable. Hang paper garlands from the ceiling, use them to frame the table, or drift them over chair backs. Suspend streamers over windows and doors like beaded curtains. Serve salad in hollowed-out melon halves, or freeze plastic novelties in ice cubes.

Have fun concentrating on the silly little details only kids would love, and everyone will have a good time. Also, encourage kids to add to the décor with their own handiwork. To rev up their excitement, enlist their help in making paper garlands and decorating the table.

party themes

During the spring and summer months, everyone loves outdoor birthday celebrations. Garden parties, pool and beach get-togethers, luaus, cookouts, picnics, tea parties, and made-to-order sundae and smoothie bars are all popular.

When the weather turns cool, shift the focus to party themes and festivities that work best indoors. At home, kids love magic or puppet shows, cupcake decorating, pizza making, or movie nights and sleepovers. In winter, have kids decorate gingerbread cookies in front of the fire or make ornaments for the holiday tree. And, if you're up for a field trip, there's always ice skating, roller skating, sledding, or bowling.

making it memorable

When the celebration comes to an end, a take-home memento is the best way for all the kids to remember the fun they had in the days ahead. And because every kid loves a good surprise, a healthy dose of creativity goes a long way toward boosting the excitement inspired by your choice of party favor, whether it be a stack of baseball cards or a beaded necklace, a colorful mask or a festive hat. A bucket overflowing with shells is a happy reminder of a beach party, a box of sidewalk chalk will continue the creativity after a art-themed party, a kerchief filled with campfire goodies tied to the end of a hobo stick offers unexpected treasures after a cookout, and a packet of daisy or vegetable seeds promises a lasting memory of a sunny tea party.

fun and festivities

Most birthday celebrations aren't complete without some type of party-oriented craft or game, or both. The most fitting crafts are those that correspond to the party's theme, such as stringing flower leis at a tiki party, decorating chocolate lollipops during a tea party, or making snow globes for a wintertime party.

Getting the kids involved in an organized game, contest, or race also helps release their birthday-party energy. Indoors, music-oriented activities, such as musical chairs, pass the parcel, and freeze dance, keep things moving. Outdoors, potato-sack and three-legged races, egg-in-a-spoon running contests, tag, and scavenger hunts are all good choices. Competitions involving limbo sticks or piñatas can take place indoors or out and are always a hit.

keeping it stress free

"Plan ahead" are the two most important words to remember. Make a list of everything you'll need for the festivities, then divide it into what can be done ahead, the day of, and during the party to ensure the event runs smoothly. Use the helpful lists provided with each party as a template for your own get-togethers. And remember, kids are great helpers, too, especially when it comes to decorations and goody bags. They'll come up with ideas that you might never have considered. Best of all, they'll take pride in their friends witnessing their contributions.

birthday cakes

The most important element of the birthday celebration is the cake. And there's no limit to the creative fun you can have in making a cake that is a perfect reflection of the birthday kid. That might mean a marble cake with whipped cream and pink sprinkles for one child, and a chocolate cake with cookie dirt and fondant bugs for another.

Deciding what kind of cake to serve can make the difference between a satisfactory and superfantastic party. A few good recipes will take care of the cake and frosting, but how you combine them and decorate the cake will make the greatest impression come party time.

layered and tiered cakes It's hard to go wrong serving a good old-fashioned layer cake for nearly any birthday celebration. Try dividing the batter into different-sized pans, then stacking the layers in tiers before frosting them, or use three small pans for a triple-layer cake. You can also save a little batter for a single cupcake to place on top, then serve it later as a special treat for the birthday kid.

making it personal A name or brief message lends individual distinction to birthday cakes. Top the cake with store-bought letters, numbers, or candies, or use a pastry (piping) bag with a plain tip (or a plastic bag with a corner snipped) to inscribe a note. Fill the bag with melted white or dark chocolate, or Decorating Icing (page 134), for particularly smooth and easy-to-write letters. Extra frosting tinted with food coloring is another good choice. Then, use your best cursive to write the cake-top message.

cake decorating

The simplest way to customize a cake is to be adventurous with your choice of fillings, frostings, and toppings. Fillings, for example, can go beyond a simple layer of icing. Try lemon curd, strawberry mousse, whipped cream, ice cream, or a fruit-laced filling (such as sliced strawberries).

Once you've stacked the layers, finish the cake with frosting or a glaze. Thicker frostings are best applied to multilayer cakes, as the heft of the frosting easily adheres to the cake sides. Swirl the frosting onto the sides first, then apply it to the cake top. Smooth glazes are a good option for single-layer cakes. Pour the glaze directly onto the top, and use an icing spatula to guide it evenly over the sides.

cake toppers For all-over toppings, shredded coconut (either plain or tinted) or chocolate curls are popular choices. (For the best results with chocolate, warm a large block in your hands, or very briefly in the microwave, then use a vegetable peeler to shave it into curls.) Other embellishments include cookies, candies, breakfast cereals, fondant cutouts, fresh edible flowers or fruit, or molded marzipan. Store-bought plastic figures and tiny toys are appealing adornments that double as take-home prizes.

icing and sprinkles Colorful frosting applied with a pastry (piping) bag is a traditional choice for decorating. For the best results, squeeze from the top of the bag with one hand, using steady pressure, and guide the tip with the other. Then add sprinkles or jimmies, applying them randomly or forming a design with a spoon or stencil.

themed cakes

With both some time and ingenuity, you can create a cake in any one of a variety of shapes and dress it up with the perfect decorations to suit your party theme.

decorations The addition of a few simple decorations is the easiest way to carry a theme. For a garden party, try tiny marzipan ladybugs, spring vegetables, or flowers nestled in a bed of chocolate-cookie dirt. For a soccer-themed party, frost a round layer cake to resemble a soccer ball, or top green "grass"–covered cupcakes (use green frosting and jimmies to create the grass) with teams of miniature players. For a kid who loves everything blue (or red or yellow), custom tint the frosting and finish with matching candles. And to celebrate any birthday with delicious style, add a cascade of layered fondant stars (page 8) or chocolate shavings and polka dots around the sides of a cake.

shaped cakes Cake pans come in many shapes and sizes. Although some of the more decorative ones can present a theme all by themselves, any traditional round or oblong cake can be transformed into a variety of profiles. A figure-eight racetrack topped with tiny cars is easily constructed from two round layers placed side by side. An edible birthday present is the outcome of square layers cut from an oblong cake, then topped with icing and wrapped with a colorful fondant bow. And, if you have another shape in mind, a sheet cake is easily trimmed to any size. (Just be sure to adjust the baking times if pan sizes differ from those specified in the recipes.)

working with fondant

Fondant, a sweet sugar paste, is most often used to form a perfectly smooth coating for cakes. It offers a wonderful surface for decorating and seals in freshness at the same time. With a texture like a very elastic pastry dough, fondant can be rolled out and cut into shapes or rIbbons for decorating, or applied in a single sheet to cover a cake completely. Look for white or tinted rolled fondant in sealed plastic bags in baking supply stores. You can also tint it at home by kneading a few drops of food coloring into white fondant.

How to use Roll out fondant on a smooth surface to a thickness of about ⅛ inch (3 mm) for covering a cake, or a thickness of about ¼ inch (6 mm) for use as decorations. As you roll, lift often to prevent sticking.

To cover a cake First, spread a thin layer of frosting on the outside of the cake. Then lay the rolled fondant over the top, gently stretching and molding it over the sides and trimming around the bottom.

To use for decorations Use cookie cutters to cut out smaller shapes. If applying the cutouts to a fondant-covered cake, brush them with water to make them sticky before placing them on the cake. Use a knife to cut out larger shapes, such as strips for tying into decorative bows. Keep any unused portions fresh by covering with a damp towel until ready to use.

ice cream

Better than a dessert sauce and more flavorful than whipped cream, nothing suits a slice of birthday cake better than the cool simplicity of ice cream.

the perfect partner Balancing the flavors of cake and ice cream can be the single detail that makes your dessert a success. As a rule of thumb, pair cakes that feature a range of flavorful ingredients (such as nuts and fruits) with plain ice creams, and simple layer cakes (like chocolate or vanilla) with more elaborately flavored ice creams.

sandwiches and sodas Some kids may choose to skip the cake altogether and focus on ice cream. For these rebels to birthday tradition, there are many options: ice cream sandwiches made with homemade cookies and covered with sprinkles, triple-scoop sundaes topped with whipped cream and chocolate sauce, homemade Creamsicles with vanilla ice cream and frozen orange or raspberry ice, layered parfaits, and old-fashioned banana splits. And for purists, an ice cream cone dipped in chocolate has no equal.

Soda fountain drinks can also be a special party treat. Set up an ice cream bar where kids can order up floats, sodas, and shakes. Keep it well stocked with 2 or 3 plain ice cream flavors, several varieties of soda, and milk. You'll also need a blender and enough long spoons, straws, and glasses for everyone. Finally, have a lot of fun garnishes on hand, such as twisty curls of citrus peel, maraschino cherries, grated chocolate, and gummi citrus wedges for rimming fruit sodas topped with vanilla ice cream.

hosting a sundae party

A make-your-own-sundae bar is a welcome alternative to a birthday cake and is a fun activity for all ages.

What you'll need Plan on 3 or 4 different ice cream flavors; chocolate, caramel, and strawberry sauces; and 8 to 10 toppings, such as Oreo cookies, chunks of peanut butter cups, M&M's, crushed candy bars, shredded coconut, gummi bears and worms, chocolate chips, jimmies, and chopped nuts; whipped cream; and maraschino cherries.

How to do it Set up a sundae bar on a table or kitchen island. Put the ice cream in the center of the bar, with the sauces in pitchers and the toppings alongside. (Keep the ice cream cold by nestling the containers in bowls of crushed ice.) Scoop the ice cream for the kids and let them do the rest.

cookies

The perfect-sized treats for kids, cookies are a welcome addition to any birthday party. Use them to adorn cakes or as take-home goodies. Decorate them in colors and styles that match the theme of the party. Make the cookies ahead of time, or involve all of the kids in baking and decorating them for a fun party activity.

fanciful cake decorations Delicious in their own right, cookies can also add snazzy three-dimensional decoration to birthday cakes. Nestle cookies into the side of frosted cakes, or stand them up in extra icing on cake tops. Try whimsically decorated sugar or gingerbread cookies, or use your own favorite cookie recipe.

party treats Fancifully decorated cookies are also wonderful for nibbling on at birthday parties, or they can be festively wrapped and toted home as a delicious reminder of the gathering. Sugar cookies are an especially good choice for decorating because they can be cut into any shape to suit the occasion, and they provide the ideal neutral canvas for a wide variety of colorful icings and toppings. Here are some ideas to try: vividly colored flower cookies for a backyard party, gingerbread cookies for a holiday-themed party, ghosts and jack-o'-lanterns for an October birthday, watermelon look-alikes for a pool party, pinwheel cookies on sticks stuck into pails of sand for a beach party, star or moon cookies for a space-themed party, or alphabet or number cookies for a kindergartner's birthday. Or, you can make simple sandwich cookies with a chocolate, peanut butter, or jam filling.

hosting a cookie party

A simple cookie exchange can be a great way to celebrate a birthday or holiday. Invite the kids to bring 1 to 2 dozen of their favorite cookies. At the party, display them all on platters and supply each kid with a jar or box in which to pack a mix to take home. Milk and hot cocoa round out the menu.

A cookie-decorating party is another favorite. Kids can help roll out the dough and then choose their favorite cookie cutters, or you can make the cookies ahead of time. Provide bowls of fun toppings and frostings, and let each kid create edible masterpieces.

One good, versatile recipe can give you lots of decorating options. Sugar or Gingerbread Cookies (pages 140 & 141) are two perfect choices. Here are a few ideas kids love.

Stained-glass cookies Cut cookie dough into 2-inch (5-cm) frames, place them on a greased baking sheet, and fill with crushed brightly colored hard candies before baking.

Pinwheel cookies Divide cookie dough into thirds and tint each with food coloring. Flatten and layer the thirds, roll, and refrigerate. Cut the chilled roll into slices and bake.

Chocolate-layer cookies Sandwich 2 baked cookies with a layer of melted chocolate, and then sprinkle with confectioners' (icing) sugar. Peanut butter and jam are also good fillings.

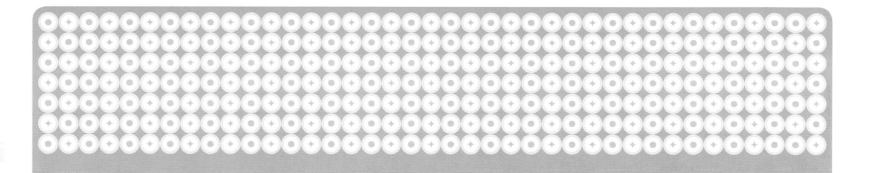

cupcake P·A·R·T·Y

An afternoon spent decorating cupcakes is the perfect way to celebrate a birthday—especially for little girls. Have lots of colorful frostings and fun toppings on hand, and leave the rest of the work to the kids! Pick a simple theme that will make the birthday celebrant smile, and plan on some old-fashioned musical games for a rousing good time.

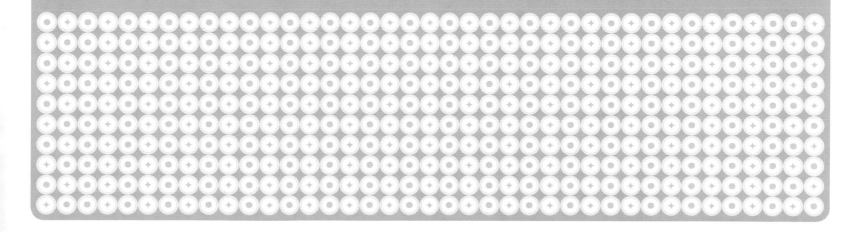

party style

invitations Send out invites that offer a touch of whimsy and introduce party themes and activities. For this occasion, a butterfly-shaped card threaded with ribbon lets everyone know that this is a girls-only party.

decorations and favors Use simple, colorful embellishments—a fanciful butterfly garland floating overhead, no-frills paper cutouts slipped onto drinking straws—that reinforce the chosen theme. Bracelets made from pastel candies add a fun dress-up element.

food Round out the menu with a selection of butterfly-shaped tea sandwiches and a pitcher of ice-cold pink lemonade. Fill the sandwiches with kids' favorites like peanut butter and jelly, tuna salad, or ham and cheese.

Fancy Finger Food For a treat that's healthy and special, pierce cubes of watermelon on fanciful party picks and arrange them on a pink pedestal and set on the table.

Colorful Cupcakes Present each guest with a sweet pink cupcake to spark creative ideas and inspiration for when the decorating begins.

Tea Sandwiches Transform everyday peanut butter and jelly into delicate tea sandwiches by cutting the bread into fun shapes with cookie cutters.

Party Decorations Add a festive touch to any party with paper garlands and dressed-up drinking straws that are so easy to do that the birthday girl can join in the fun of decorating.

cupcake party • 27

Pretty Place Cards Flower-shaped fans do double duty as place cards and party favors. Add flourish to the name tags by cutting with pinking shears.

Colorful Toppings A variety of sweet toppings in a palette of colors is the way to go for any cupcake-decorating party. Pastel frosting is the perfect canvas for sprinkles and candies.

Party Hair Clips Attach paper butterflies to plain hair clips to enhance a party theme—and make fun takeaway gifts.

Fanciful Beverages Frilly straws, fresh strawberry slices, and pink-sugared rims make these drinks special. To coat the rims, first rub them with a lemon wedge, then dip them in sugar before filling with brightly hued lemonade.

party plan

overall strategy Make the cupcakes and frostings in advance of the party day. Decorate a few of the cupcakes ahead of time to give the kids some creative ideas, then let them finish off the rest during the celebration with a generous supply of plain cupcakes, frostings, and decorations to choose from.

what to serve With kids dipping their fingers into frostings, candies, and cupcakes during most of the party, balance the menu with more nutritious offerings, such as kid-sized sandwiches and fresh fruit.

serving suggestions Transform the ordinary into the extraordinary! Make sandwiches shaped like butterflies and serve them on a pedestal. Rim the glasses with colored sugar. Pierce bite-sized cubes of fresh watermelon with decorative toothpicks.

recipes

Vanilla Cupcakes with
Vanilla Frosting

○●○

Chocolate Cupcakes with
Chocolate Frosting

ahead of time

parents
- Send or hand out invitations.
- Purchase all of the ingredients and/or make party decorations.
- Make the batter and bake the cupcakes.
- Make the beverage.

kids
- Help with the decorations.

day of the party

parents
- Make the sandwiches and frostings.
- Decorate the party room and set a table for the number of guests attending.
- Decorate an extra cupcake for each guest. Wrap some for party favors, and reserve some as examples.
- Prepare a special table for cupcake decorating. Set out the remaining frosted cupcakes along with small bowls filled with decorations.

kids
- Help decorate.
- Frost the cupcakes.

during the party

parents
- Give kids ideas and examples for decorating cupcakes.
- Assist kids in party games.
- Box cupcakes for party favors.

kids
- Decorate the cupcakes and have fun!

activity ideas

Musical Chairs Get the kids up and moving with a round of musical chairs, freeze dance, or another heart-pumping activity. Tying balloons to chair backs makes the game a bit more challenging.

Balloon Stomp Tie balloons on ankles and let the stomp begin. The last one with an unpopped balloon is the winner.

Pass the Parcel Pass a wrapped present as music plays. Each time the music stops, the kid with the present unwraps it to reveal another (smaller) parcel, until the last child finds a prize.

decorating cupcakes

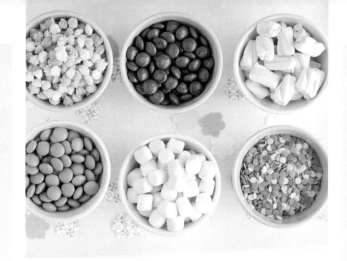

There is no end to the number of toppings and delicious decorations the intrepid cupcake decorator can use. An assortment of colorful candies, such as the marshmallows, nonpareils, M&M's, and sprinkles used here, is a must.

But a wide range of other options exists, too: pastry (piping) bags fitted with a selection of tips and filled with a variety of colored frostings, stencils (cookie cutters work well) and colored sugars, and small figures and toys that double as party favors. Think about your party theme or occasion when choosing decorations. And be sure to have some decorated cupcakes on hand to boost creativity!

creative ideas and tips

● Younger kids will be happy using just colorful sprinkles to decorate, but older kids will enjoy creating more elaborate designs.

● Drizzle icing in a contrasting color over the top of the frosted cupcake, and cut through it with a knife to make designs.

● Cut cookies, fondant, gels, or gummi candies into shapes for dressing up cupcake tops.

● Use stencils and different-colored sugars to make simple designs on cupcake tops.

● Giving each party guest a pretty decorated cupcake to take home is a fun way to commemorate the occasion. Make a bed of soft miniature marshmallows in a small box, then nestle the cupcake in the marshmallows to keep it from getting squished on the way home. Seal the packages with a colored silk or grosgrain ribbon with a fanciful paper cutout.

These yummy kid-sized cakes can be baked up to 2 days in advance and stored covered with plastic wrap at room temperature. But wait until the day of the party to frost them.

Makes 12 cupcakes

. . . .

All-purpose (plain) flour 1½ cups
(7½ oz/235 g)

Baking powder 2 teaspoons

Salt large pinch

Unsalted butter ½ cup (4 oz/125 g),
at room temperature

Sugar 1 cup (8 oz/250 g)

Vanilla extract (essence) 1 teaspoon

Large eggs 2, at room temperature

Whole milk ¾ cup (6 fl oz/180 ml),
at room temperature

Vanilla Frosting (page 132) ½ recipe

Vanilla Cupcakes

⬦ Preheat the oven to 350°F (180°C). Line a 12-cup muffin pan with paper liners.

⬦ In a bowl, stir together the flour, baking powder, and salt. Set aside.

⬦ In a large bowl, using a handheld mixer or a stand mixer fitted with the paddle attachment, beat together the butter, sugar, and vanilla on medium speed until creamy, about 3 minutes. Add the eggs, one at a time, beating well after each addition. Stop the mixer and scrape down the sides of the bowl using a rubber spatula. On low speed, beat in the flour mixture in 3 additions alternately with the milk in 2 additions, beginning and ending with the flour mixture and beating just until blended after each addition.

⬦ Pour the batter into the prepared muffin cups, filling each cup about three-fourths full. Bake until golden and a toothpick inserted into the center of a cupcake comes out clean, 17–20 minutes. Let cool in the pan on a wire rack for 5 minutes, then remove the cupcakes from the pan and let cool completely on the rack. Frost the cooled cupcakes.

Marble Cupcakes Variation In a small bowl, stir together ¼ cup (2 fl oz/60 ml) hot water and ¼ cup (¾ oz/20 g) unsweetened cocoa powder. Make the vanilla cupcake batter as directed. Spoon 1¾ cups (14 fl oz/430 ml) of the batter into a bowl, and stir in the cocoa mixture until blended. Working with 1 prepared muffin cup at a time, spoon enough of the vanilla batter into one side of the cup to fill it almost halfway, and then spoon enough of the chocolate batter into the other side of the cup to fill it about four-fifths full. (You may have enough batter left over for an extra cupcake or two.) Bake the cupcakes as directed above.

These dense, chocolatey miniature cakes are a kid favorite. Top the frosting with chocolate sprinkles for a triple dose of chocolate. Or, substitute Vanilla Frosting (page 132) tinted the color of your choice.

Chocolate Cupcakes

● Preheat the oven to 350°F (180°C). Line a 12-cup muffin pan with paper liners.

● In a bowl, stir together the flour, baking powder, and salt. Set aside. Pour the boiling water into a small bowl, and whisk in the cocoa powder. Set aside.

● In a large bowl, using a handheld mixer or a stand mixer fitted with the paddle attachment, beat together the butter, sugar, and vanilla on medium speed until creamy, about 3 minutes. Add the eggs, one at a time, beating well after each addition. Stop the mixer and scrape down the sides of the bowl using a rubber spatula. On low speed, beat in the flour mixture in 3 additions alternately with the milk in 2 additions, beginning and ending with the flour mixture and beating just until blended after each addition. Using the spatula, stir in the chocolate mixture until blended.

● Pour the batter into the muffin cups, filling each cup about four-fifths full. Bake until a toothpick inserted into the center of a cupcake comes out clean, 20–25 minutes. Let cool in the pan on a wire rack for 5 minutes, then remove the cupcakes from the pan and let cool completely on the rack. Frost the cooled cupcakes.

Make-Ahead Tip The cupcakes can be baked up to 2 days in advance, covered with plastic wrap, and stored at room temperature. Frost them the day of the party.

Makes 12 cupcakes

All-purpose (plain) flour 1½ cups (7½ oz/235 g)

Baking powder 1 tablespoon

Salt pinch

Boiling water ½ cup (4 fl oz/125 ml)

Unsweetened cocoa powder ½ cup (1½ oz/45 g)

Unsalted butter ½ cup (4 oz/125 g), at room temperature

Sugar 1 cup (8 oz/250 g)

Vanilla extract (essence) 1 teaspoon

Large eggs 2, at room temperature

Whole milk ¾ cup (6 fl oz/180 ml), at room temperature

Chocolate Frosting (page 132) ½ recipe

easter P·A·R·T·Y

A grassy lawn makes a perfect setting for an Easter celebration fit for kids of all ages. Hide dyed eggs among the hedges and let the party guests hunt high and low before they settle on blankets to eat and compare finds. Help the kids decorate baskets and eggs, or make daisy chains. A round of lawn games and races complete the day's activities.

party style

invitations Create invitations that evoke the joyful feel of this spring holiday. A card shaped like an egg or a daisy, and embellished with colorful ribbon or stickers, conveys the sweet playfulness of the gathering.

decorations and favors Carry the occasion's colors—grassy green, yellow gingham, robin's egg blue, bright white—onto the table and beyond. Use baskets to hold everything from napkins to nosegays to little chicks.

food Put together an Easter-inspired buffet including baby carrots with stems attached, ham and cheese sandwiches on small rolls or tucked into pita, and deviled eggs. Save the sweets (chocolate eggs, jelly beans, and lollipops) for the take-home baskets.

Melon Balls Dress up this everyday treat by serving it in a scallop-edged watermelon bowl. A mix of green honeydew and golden watermelon delivers a fresh and inviting look.

Nest of Eggs Nestle Easter eggs (dyed in light blues and greens and decorated with polka dots and flowers) in a footed bowl filled with straw.

Easter Baskets Personalize baskets with a patterned satin or grosgrain ribbon and fill with garden-inspired treats, like a cluster of daisies, a toy rabbit, and a packet of seeds.

Buffet Setup Set the table to match the scene. Use a gingham tablecloth, garlands of fresh daisies, and plates and cutlery that are outdoor-friendly.

Flower Garland Celebrate springtime's flowery display with a handmade garland made of garden-fresh daisies. Let kids weave the chains themselves with a few helpful tips from you.

Spring Buffet Make the buffet table easy to navigate with plates stacked on one end and utensils wrapped in napkins and sealed with pretty ribbons.

Garden Cupcakes Carrot cupcakes are the perfect choice for Easter. For seasonal charm, dress up each cupcake with a spring vegetable or flower made from marzipan or fondant.

Fresh Lemonade Markets are stocked with lemons in spring, so fill a punch bowl with just-squeezed lemonade. Sprigs of mint add a refreshing scent.

party plan

overall strategy Once the food is prepared and arranged on the buffet table, shift the focus to lawn games and other fun outdoor activities.

what to serve Easter calls for sweet treats, but serve them alongside savory items like ham and cheese spiked with honey mustard and nestled in soft dinner rolls, or deviled eggs.

serving suggestions Think spring. Adorn the buffet and platters with fresh flowers and pastel-tinted eggs. Garnish with sprigs of mint and lemon slices. Top the cupcakes with fanciful garden-inspired treats.

recipes

Fresh-Squeezed Lemonade

Melon Ball Salad

Easter Egg Lollipops

Garden-Top Carrot Cupcakes
with Cream Cheese Frosting

ahead of time

parents
- Make the cupcakes and frosting.
- Decorate the Easter baskets.
- Make the lemonade.
- Wrap utensils in napkins for the buffet.

kids
- Help decorate the Easter baskets.
- Squeeze lemons for the lemonade.

day of the party

parents
- Frost and decorate the cupcakes.
- Make the salad.
- Make sandwiches, deviled eggs, or other dishes to serve as part of the buffet.
- Organize and decorate the buffet table.
- Assemble a table with lollipop sticks and decorations for making the lollipops.
- Set out games—croquet, hula hoops, jump ropes—in areas where kids will easily find and use them; hide the eggs for the hunt.

kids
- Pick flowers and weave to make garlands.
- Help scoop melon balls for the salad.

during the party

parents
- Help kids make the lollipops.
- Rally and organize kids for lawn games.
- Replenish the buffet as needed.

kids
- Play games, hunt for eggs, and make the lollipops.

activity ideas

Lawn Games Outdoor games are key to Easter fun. Try egg-in-a-spoon relay races, croquet, badminton, an egg toss, Simon says, a bean bag toss, or a race to see who can be first to push an egg over a finish line...with his or her nose!

Easter Favors Think favors that double as activities, such as bubble-blowing liquid and wands, and baskets for decorating with ribbons, flowers, and toys.

Egg Hunt No Easter party is complete without one. Don't skimp on the hidden treasures and prizes!

decorating egg lollipops

At Easter time, nothing inspires creativity better than a snow white egg—and in this case, it's an egg made of melted white chocolate—ready for some colorful springtime touches. First, pipe streams or dots of pastel-colored melted chocolate from disposable pastry (piping) bags (or plastic sandwich bags with a corner snipped off) onto the lollipops.

Next, while the chocolate is still soft, add the decorations, pressing them down to stay in place. If the piping chocolate begins to harden, seal the tip of the bag with a paper clip and slip the bag into a bowl of hot water, or put the bag in the microwave for 10 seconds, or just until softened.

creative ideas and tips

- Look for candies and sprinkles in the full range of spring colors for an appealing palette.

- Miniature candies, white chocolate chips, sliced gumdrops, jelly beans, or tiny nonpareils are all good additions to your table of sweet and colorful decorations.

- For three-dimensional decorations, tint marzipan in pastel colors and cut or mold into Easter-inspired shapes, such as flowers, carrots, fruits, chicks, and bunnies.

- Set out jimmies and other tiny candy shapes for sprinkling with fingertips onto the soft chocolate.

- Slip extra lollipops into clear cellophane bags, tie with raffia or ribbon, and pair each bag with a fresh flower to send home as party favors.

- Fill small baskets with soft tufts of clipped wheatgrass and stand any extra lollipops in the grass. They'll look like a collection of beautiful Easter eggs waiting to be discovered.

Fresh-Squeezed Lemonade

Serves 8

Fresh lemon juice 1⅓ cups
(11 fl oz/340 ml)

Superfine (caster) sugar 1⅓ cups
(10 oz/315 g)

Cold water 6 cups (48 fl oz/1.5 l)

Ice

Thin lemon slices 8, for garnish
(optional)

● Pour the lemon juice into a 2-qt (2-l) pitcher. Add the sugar and stir until dissolved. Stir in the water. Cover and refrigerate until serving. (The lemonade can be made up to 4 days in advance.)

● To serve, fill tall glasses with ice and pour in the lemonade. Garnish each glass with a lemon slice, if desired.

Pink Lemonade Variation To make pink lemonade, stir 5–6 drops red food coloring into the lemonade before serving.

Melon Ball Salad

Serves 8

Melons 2, of different varieties

Fresh lime or orange juice
1 tablespoon

Lime or orange zest
½ teaspoon finely grated

● Using a sharp knife, cut off the top one-third of the largest melon. Scoop out and discard the seeds from both pieces. Then, using a melon baller, scoop melon balls from both the top one-third and the bottom two-thirds into a large bowl, removing all of the flesh but leaving sturdy walls intact in the bottom portion. Remove about half of the balls to a second bowl, cover, and refrigerate for another use. With the knife, attractively trim the rim of the melon "bowl," creating a scalloped or sawtoothed edge. Set the melon bowl aside. Cut the remaining melon in half, and remove and discard the seeds. Scoop out balls from the melon halves and add them to the bowl holding the other balls. You should have about 6 cups (2¼ lb/1.1 kg).

● Add the juice and zest to the melon balls and stir gently to mix. Gently scoop the melon balls into the melon bowl. Serve at once, or cover and refrigerate for up to 6 hours before serving.

When it is time for the partygoers to assemble their lollipops, each one of them will need a lollipop stick and a sheet of waxed paper. Review the ideas on page 47 before you begin.

Easter Egg Lollipops

Pour the chocolate chips into a heatproof bowl and set over (not touching) simmering water in a saucepan. Heat, stirring occasionally, until melted and smooth, about 5 minutes. You will have 1 cup (8 fl oz/250 ml) melted chocolate. Plan on using 1 generous tablespoon-sized dollop of melted chocolate for each lollipop.

Color half of the melted chocolate for decorating: For each color, spoon about 3 tablespoons melted chocolate into a small bowl. Add 1 drop of food coloring and stir until blended. Spoon the tinted chocolate into a sturdy resealable plastic bag and secure closed, or into a disposable pastry (piping) bag, twist the top closed, and secure with a rubber band. Place the filled portion of the bag in a small bowl of hot water so the chocolate doesn't harden. Repeat to color more batches of chocolate.

Give each child a small sheet of waxed paper and place a lollipop stick on top. Remove the melted chocolate reserved for making the lollipops from over the hot water. Let each child spoon a dollop over the top of the stick, and then use the spoon to spread the chocolate into an oval about 2 by 3½ inches (5 by 9 cm). Twist the stick gently to coat it with chocolate. The stick should extend from the middle of the oval. Carefully dry the bags of colored chocolate and snip the ends to create small holes for piping. Have the children pipe designs onto their eggs and decorate with candies and/or sprinkles, if they wish. Once decorated, let dry until firm, about 15 minutes. Peel away the waxed paper and enjoy!

Makes 8 lollipops

White chocolate chips 1 bag
(11 oz/345 g)

Food coloring 3 colors of choice

Small candies and/or sprinkles for decorating (optional)

All-purpose (plain) flour 2¼ cups
(11½ oz/360 g)

Light brown sugar 1½ cups
(10½ oz/330 g) firmly packed

Baking powder 1 tablespoon

Ground cinnamon 1 teaspoon

Salt ½ teaspoon

Grated carrots 1½ cups (9 oz/280 g)

Vegetable oil ¾ cup (6 fl oz/180 ml)

Large eggs 4, at room temperature

Vanilla extract (essence) 1½ teaspoons

Finely chopped walnuts ¾ cup
(3 oz/90 g), optional

Makes about 1½ cups
(12 fl oz/375 ml)

Cream cheese 4 oz (125 g),
at room temperature

Unsalted butter 6 tablespoons
(3 oz/90 g), at room temperature

Vanilla extract (essence) 1 teaspoon

Confectioners' (icing) sugar 2 cups
(8 oz/250 g)

Garden-Top Carrot Cupcakes

● Preheat the oven to 325°F (165°C). Line 18 muffin pan cups with paper liners.

● In a large bowl, stir together the flour, brown sugar, baking powder, cinnamon, and salt. In a small bowl, combine the carrots, oil, eggs, and vanilla and stir until blended. Stir the carrot mixture into the flour mixture just until blended. Stir in the nuts, if using.

● Pour the batter into the prepared muffin cups. Bake until a toothpick inserted into the center of a cupcake comes out clean, 16–18 minutes. Let cool in the pans on a wire rack for 5 minutes, then remove and let cool on the rack. The cupcakes can be made up to 3 days in advance and refrigerated in an airtight container. Frost them the day of the party.

Garden Toppers Use tinted and shaped marzipan and/or fondant to create decorations with a garden theme. The rough surface of fresh kale leaves can be used to form leaflike impressions. Make the toppers up to a day in advance and store in an airtight container.

Layer Cake Variation Divide the batter between 2 buttered and floured 9-inch (23-cm) round cake pans and bake for 30 to 40 minutes. Double the frosting recipe.

Cream Cheese Frosting

● In a large bowl, using a handheld mixer or a stand mixer fitted with the paddle attachment, beat together the cream cheese, butter, and vanilla on medium speed until smooth, about 2 minutes. Stop the mixer and scrape down the sides of the bowl with a rubber spatula. With the mixer on low speed, gradually beat in half of the confectioners' sugar until incorporated. Use at once, or cover and refrigerate for up to 2 days.

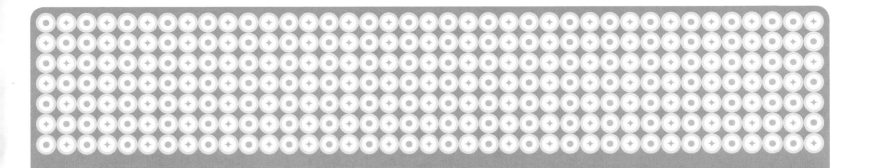

backyard P·A·R·T·Y

Kids don't have to travel far for a great party destination. Cover the old picnic tables, bring in some hay bales for seating and a fire pit for roasting marshmallows, and let the fun begin. Swinging at a piñata and going on a scavenger hunt provide active challenges for all ages. As the sun sets, tell ghost stories inside a dimly lit makeshift teepee.

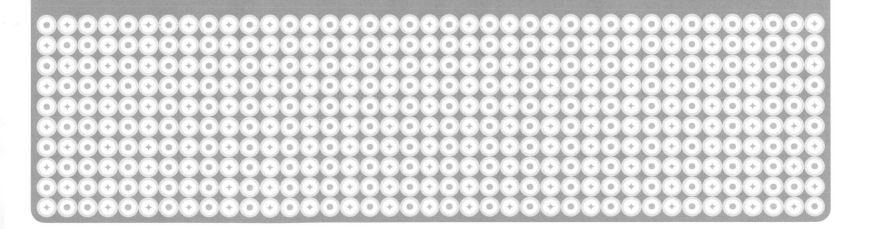

party style

invitations Check scrapbooking and art-supply stores for checked or rustic paisley papers for framing printed cards. Attach tiny die-cut hot dogs, harmonicas, straw hats, or corncobs to the cards for a finishing touch.

decorations and favors Any backyard gains country appeal with plenty of gingham and colorful bandanas, hay bales for sitting on, and a fire pit for roasting sausages and marshmallows. Straw hats and hobo sticks with bundles of campfire paraphernalia make great mementos.

food Backyard cooking is kid food at its best: large bowls brimming with sweet-and-salty Chex mix, grilled or fire-roasted sausages, and rich, gooey s'mores. Iced herbal tea and fruit punch provide cooling refreshment.

Grilled Fruit Wedges of grilled peach or other summer stone fruits offer a light alternative to roasted marshmallows. Skewer and grill, or roast the wedges on a stick over the fire.

Bell Jar Glassware Jars that double as drinking glasses were common in farmhouse kitchens of the past. A gingham sash adds country charm.

All the Fixings Keep each table stocked with everything kids need to doll up their sausages and, later, their s'mores. Herbal iced tea or lemonade poured from spigot jars sitting atop hay bales make self-service a snap.

Banner Finish Line A gingham party banner doubles as an impromptu finish line for potato-sack races or outdoor relays.

Hobo-Stick Bundles Gather party favors into colorful kerchiefs and tie onto sticks for kids to sling over their shoulders like wayward hobos. Inside, include items for an evening by the campfire.

Fun Favors Kid-sized binoculars and a canteen assist in backyard adventures, while a harmonica and songbook come in handy when the singing begins.

Perfect Picnic Find a shady clearing for the table. A bright gingham tablecloth and tree-strung banner mark the picnic spot enticingly. Paper liners laid over the tablecloth simplify cleanup.

Corn Butters Sweet or savory butters add appeal to corn on the cob. Make the butters well ahead, then bring to room temperature before serving.

party plan

overall strategy Have kids work up an appetite with outdoor-themed games before sitting down by the fire to cook sausages and marshmallows. After the meal, a piñata offers everyone the chance for a prize.

what to serve Focus on food that cooks on a grill or over an open flame. Balance the menu with some dishes that can be prepared ahead in the kitchen, then added to the outdoor buffet at mealtime.

serving suggestions Offer plastic, bamboo, or melamine plates and glassware for outdoor dining. Make drinks and condiments readily accessible so kids can easily help themselves.

recipes

Chex Mix

Corn on the Cobettes

Fire-Roasted Sausages on Sticks

S'mores

ahead of time

parents
- Choose a safe space outdoors for building a fire or setting up a firepit or grill.
- Arrange seating around the fire so everyone has plenty of room.
- Make the flavored butters and the beverages and help kids with the Chex Mix.
- Assemble hobo bundles.

kids
- Find some good clean sticks, or long skewers, for roasting marshmallows.
- Make the Chex Mix.

day of the party

parents
- Assemble graham crackers, chocolates, and marshmallows for s'mores.
- Assemble condiments for the sausages.
- Set up a serving table with stations for sausage fixings and s'more ingredients.
- Cook the corn. Make any other side dishes or accompaniments that do not require outdoor cooking.
- Soak wooden skewers in water.

kids
- Help parents stack wood for the fire.

during the party

parents
- Establish fire-safety rules and supervise all fire roasting.
- Assist kids with games and activities.

kids
- Work on your fire-roasting technique.

activity ideas

Outdoor Races Potato sack races, three-legged races, a scavenger hunt, and an obstacle course are all good choices for giggle-inducing backyard activities.

Campfire Fun Since campfires inspire their own special camaraderie, try a round of favorite songs, a few scary ghost stories, or a game of hot potato while gathered around the fire.

Piñata Play Piñatas are great for all ages. Fill a fun-shaped piñata with prizes and line up the kids from smallest to biggest. A bat or heavy stick does the trick.

making s'mores

There is a specific, timeworn technique to making the perfect rendition of this ubiquitous campfire favorite, a hit with partygoers of all ages. First, marshmallows are best roasted over glowing embers, rather than a flame, so let your fire die out a bit in areas before you begin.

Next, present the fixings. Offer more choices than the traditional s'more ingredients: various chocolate bars, flavored or rough-cut marshmallows, and spiced graham crackers all add a contemporary touch to this tried-and-true fire-roasted confection.

creative ideas and tips

● Give in to your worst (best!) impulses when assembling your s'more ingredients and offer lots of delicious options.

● Include plain milk, semisweet, and white chocolate bars; peanut butter cups; chocolate-covered caramels; crispy rice chocolate bars; almond chocolate bars; chocolate-mint patties; and hazelnut-chocolate spread.

● Offer plain, cinnamon, and chocolate-covered graham crackers, split in half.

● Try plain, coconut-coated, and chocolate-covered marshmallows.

● To build the fire, try a tepee technique: Crumple 4 or 5 pieces of newspaper into a mound and stand small pieces of wood (kindling) on top of the mound in a tepee shape. Arrange logs over the kindling in the tepee shape. Light the paper and, with luck, the kindling and the logs will ignite. If the flames begin to die, use a food-safe starter fluid to keep them going. Do not leave the fire unattended at any time.

This sweet-salty Chex-cereal mix is a party must-have and a hit with all ages. Substitute your favorites—bagel chips, pumpkin seeds, raisins, dried cranberries—for the nuts, pretzels, and/or crackers.

Serves 12

• • • • • • • • • • • • • •

Unsalted butter 4 tablespoons
(2 oz/60 g)

Worcestershire sauce
1½ tablespoons

Sugar 2 teaspoons

Seasoned salt 1 teaspoon

Onion powder ½ teaspoon

Garlic powder ¼ teaspoon

**Chex cereal, in any combination
of wheat, rice, and/or corn chex**
4 cups (6 oz/185 g)

Mixed nuts ½ cup (2½ oz/75 g)

Bite-sized pretzels ½ cup
(2½ oz/75 g)

**Bite-sized Cheddar crackers,
Cheddar cracker sticks, or Cheddar
Goldfish crackers** ½ cup (2½ oz/75 g)

Chex Mix

● Preheat the oven to 250°F (120°C). Put the butter in a shallow baking dish and set in the oven just until melted. Stir in the Worcestershire sauce, sugar, seasoned salt, onion powder, and garlic powder until well blended. Add the cereal, nuts, pretzels, and crackers and toss gently but thoroughly to coat with the seasoned butter. Spread the mixture evenly in the dish.

● Bake, stirring every 10 minutes, until crisp, about 45 minutes. Let cool completely. Serve immediately, or store in an airtight container at room temperature for up to 1 week.

Serve the flavored butters in crocks alongside the corn, and let kids smear them to taste. They can be made up to 1 week in advance, covered, and refrigerated. Bring to room temperature before serving.

Corn on the Cobettes

● Bring a large saucepan three-fourths full of water to a boil. Meanwhile, cut each ear of corn into 3 equal pieces. Add the corn to the boiling water and boil until the kernels are tender when pierced with a fork, 5–7 minutes. Using tongs, transfer the corn to a platter. Serve hot or at room temperature with the flavored butters alongside.

Roasted Garlic Butter Preheat the oven to 400°F (200°C). Cut off the top one-third of the garlic head. Place the head, cut side up, on a piece of aluminum foil, drizzle the oil over the top, and seal the head inside the foil. Roast until the cloves are soft, about 25 minutes. Unwrap, let cool slightly, then squeeze the cloves from their papery sheaths into a small bowl. Add the butter and mix with a fork until blended.

Maple Butter In a small bowl, combine the butter and maple syrup and mix with a fork until blended.

Cinnamon Spice Butter In a small bowl, stir together the cinnamon and sugar. Add the butter and mix with a fork until blended.

Pecan Butter In a small bowl, stir together the pecans and sugar. Add the butter and mix with a fork until blended.

Serves 12

Ears of corn 4, husks and silk removed

FLAVORED BUTTERS

Salted butter 4 tablespoons (2 oz/60 g), at room temperature, for each butter

ROASTED GARLIC BUTTER

Garlic 1 large head

Olive oil 1 teaspoon

MAPLE BUTTER

Maple syrup 1½ teaspoon

CINNAMON SPICE BUTTER

Ground cinnamon 1 teaspoon

Granulated sugar ½ teaspoon

PECAN BUTTER

Toasted pecans 2 tablespoons finely chopped

Light brown sugar 2 teaspoons firmly packed

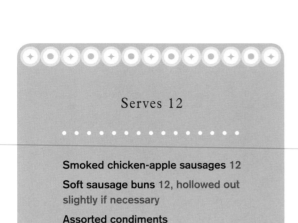

Serves 12

· · · · · · · · · · · · · ·

Smoked chicken-apple sausages 12

Soft sausage buns 12, hollowed out slightly if necessary

Assorted condiments

Fire-Roasted Sausages on Sticks

● Build a fire in a fire pit (page 63), or prepare a fire in a gas or charcoal grill for direct-heat grilling over medium heat. Outfit each kid with a long stick with a tapered end or a campfire skewer at least 2 feet (60 cm) long. (A straightened wire coat hanger also works well.) Pierce each sausage through its center with the end of the stick or skewer.

● When the fire is ready, let kids hold the sausages over the fire, turning them often, until browned and smoky, 4–5 minutes. Then, with each sausage still on its stick or skewer, have them poke the sausage right into a bun and, holding the sausage by both sides of the bun, pull the stick out of the sausage. Serve hot with the condiments.

Suggested Condiments Shredded Monterey jack or Cheddar cheese, sauerkraut, thin red onion slices, thin tomato slices, pickle relish, mustard, mayonnaise, ketchup.

Makes 24

· · · · · · · · · · · · · ·

Large marshmallows 24

Semisweet (plain) or milk chocolate 6 bars (1½ oz/45 g each), broken into quarters

Whole regular or cinnamon graham crackers 24, each broken into 2 squares

S'mores

● Pierce a marshmallow onto the tip of a campfire stick (see recipe above). When the fire has died down to a glow, let the kids hold the marshmallows over the embers and roast them, turning them constantly, until golden brown on all sides, 3–4 minutes.

● To make each s'more, place a piece of chocolate on a graham cracker square, top with a roasted marshmallow, set a second graham cracker square on top, and squish the marshmallow and chocolate together to make a gooey sandwich.

Variations Use 24 miniature peanut butter cups or miniature chocolate mint patties in place of the chocolate, or use a mixture of both. For more ideas, see page 63.

tiki P·A·R·T·Y

A sun-filled celebration feels like a tropical vacation when it includes pretty flower leis, grass skirts, made-to-order smoothies, fresh tropical fruit, grilled Hawaiian kebabs, and a quick lesson in hula and limbo (have the kids help out by holding the pole). Fun for kids of all ages, this festive party is great by a pool, at the beach, or on a lawn.

party style

invitations Island-themed parties inspire plenty of ideas. Try a rolled-up "message" in a cork-topped bottle (page 77). Or, make or buy cards that picture hula dancers, tiki totems, or tropical fruit or flowers.

decorations Tropical flowers—whether fresh or made from paper streamers or crêpe paper—add a colorful, festive note to everything from hair clips and leis to napkin rings and limbo poles. Set bamboo torches blazing with bright orange and yellow tissue-paper flames.

food Fresh tropical fruits—on skewers, in smoothies, as a design for cookies—are a kid favorite. Grilled chicken kebabs are the savory centerpiece of the menu. For dessert, serve coconut or macadamia nut cookies.

Party Favors Make-it-yourself flower leis are a natural choice. Or, fill beach buckets with sand, shells, flip-flops, fruity candies, paper umbrellas, or other island-inspired items.

Island Games A limbo contest tests flexibility, but kids will also be game for pass-the-torch relay races, a tiki treasure hunt, or a round of hula freeze dance.

Smoothie Bar Equip a table with a blender and glasses for made-to-order smoothies. Stock it with bowls of fresh-cut fruits, carafes of juice, and lots of vanilla yogurt and ice.

Tiki Totem A watermelon makes an ideal surface for carving a totem to set on the serving table. At night, use a candle to illuminate the face.

Island Music Set the mood with the sounds of Caribbean steel drums, Hawaiian hula, Jamaican reggae, or other island rhythms.

Tropical Flourishes Cut fresh tropical fruit into fanciful shapes that kids can string onto skewers. Paper hibiscus blooms adorn napkins, while colorful crazy straws make for fun sipping.

party plan

overall strategy Make the dipping sauce
and marinade, and ready all smoothie and skewer
ingredients ahead of time. At the party, one adult
can make smoothies, while the other tends the grill.

what to serve Build on the island theme. Taro
chips or Maui onion rings whet the appetite for
smoothies. Steamed rice studded with macadamia
nuts and toasted coconut makes a nice complement
to chicken skewers.

serving suggestions Use edible, pesticide-free
tropical flowers in abundance on plates and tables,
and as adornments for glassware.

recipes

Fruit Smoothies

Lava Flows

Hawaiian Chicken Kebabs

Mango Dipping Sauce

ahead of time

parents ● Make the dipping sauce.

● Cut up the chicken and pineapple. Make
the basting sauce. Cover and refrigerate all
in separate containers until ready to use.

● Cut up fruit for the fresh fruit skewers,
cover, and refrigerate.

● Island music will set the theme and mood.
Select some for the party day.

kids ● Help parents cut fruit into fun shapes for
the smoothie garnishes and fruit skewers.

day of the party

parents ● Soak wooden skewers used for grilling.

● Assemble the chicken kebabs.

● Designate a smoothie-making station and
outfit with all the ingredients you'll need.
A small refrigerator or cooler will help keep
ice and ingredients cold.

kids ● Help parents set up and decorate.

during the party

parents ● If the party includes swimming, have a
lifeguard or other adult on duty at all times.

● Make the blended drinks to order.

● Grill the chicken kebabs.

kids ● Make flower leis or other tropical crafts.

● Thread fresh fruit onto skewers.

● Order the smoothie of your choice.

activity ideas

Learn to Hula Whether it's with hula hoops or skirts (or both), hula dancing is fun at any tropical-themed party. Look to the pros or how-to DVDs for guidance.

Flower Leis Tissue-paper flowers strung with shells or beads are a great (and less expensive) alternative to fresh-flower leis. They're easy to make and durable, too!

Fruit Skewers While an adult is busy blending smoothies, the party guests can make their own fresh-fruit swizzle sticks. Offer tropical fruit slices and thin bamboo skewers for piercing them.

Fruit Smoothies

Put the ice in a blender. Break each banana into quarters and add to the blender. Add the mango, yogurt, orange juice, and milk and process until smooth. You should have 6 cups (48 fl oz/1.5 l). Divide the mixture evenly among 6 glasses and serve at once.

Variations For a thicker smoothie, use frozen mango cubes or add more ice. For a smoothie more akin to a milk shake, use half-and-half (half cream) instead of milk.

Serves 6

Ice cubes 1 cup (8 oz/250 g)

Bananas 2, peeled

Fresh or thawed frozen mango cubes 4 cups (1½ lb/740 g)

Low-fat vanilla yogurt ¾ cup (6 oz/185 g)

Fresh orange juice 1 cup (8 fl oz/250 ml)

Whole milk ¼ cup (2 fl oz/60 ml)

Lava Flows

Put the ice in a blender. Break each banana into quarters and add to the blender. Add the pineapple juice, milk, and coconut cream and process until smooth. You should have 6 cups (48 fl oz/1.5 l).

Divide the strawberries evenly among 6 glasses. Divide the blended mixture evenly among the glasses, pouring it into each glass with a great gush so the strawberries swirl decoratively. If desired, garnish each glass with a strawberry half speared on a skewer.

Serves 6

Ice cubes 2 cups (1 lb/500 g)

Bananas 2, peeled

Pineapple juice 1½ cups (12 fl oz/375 ml)

Whole milk 1 cup (8 fl oz/250 ml)

Coconut cream 3 tablespoons

Thawed frozen sweetened sliced strawberries 1½ cups (8 oz/235 g), coarsely chopped

Fresh whole large strawberries 3, hulled and halved lengthwise (optional)

Pineapple juice ½ cup (4 fl oz/125 ml)

Olive oil 3 tablespoons, plus more for brushing

Soy sauce 2 tablespoons

Light brown sugar 2 tablespoons

Shallot 1 tablespoon minced

Fresh ginger 1 tablespoon peeled and grated

Garlic 1 clove, finely minced

Boneless, skinless chicken breast halves 3 (about 1½ lb/.75 kg total), cut into 1½-inch (4-cm) cubes

Pineapple ½, peeled, cored, and cut into 1-inch (2.5-cm) cubes

Serves 6–8

Yellow onion 1, finely diced

Olive oil 3 tablespoons

Mangoes 2, peeled and finely diced

Fresh orange juice ½ cup (4 fl oz/125 ml)

Garlic 2 cloves, finely minced

Lime 1, juiced

Honey 2 tablespoons

Hawaiian Chicken Kebabs

● Prepare a fire in a gas or charcoal grill for direct-heat grilling over medium heat. If using wooden skewers, soak 12–16 skewers in water to cover for at least 15 minutes.

● In a small bowl, combine the pineapple juice, oil, soy sauce, sugar, shallot, ginger, and garlic. Stir to mix well to make a basting sauce. (The basting sauce and the cut-up chicken and pineapple can be refrigerated in separate containers up to 1 day in advance).

● Thread the chicken pieces alternately with the pineapple pieces onto 12–16 skewers. Brush both the chicken and pineapple lightly with oil. (The assembled kebabs can be covered and refrigerated for up to 3 hours. Bring to room temperature before grilling.)

● Brush the kebabs liberally with some of the basting sauce. Oil the grill rack. Grill the kebabs, basting them frequently with the sauce and turning them with tongs as needed, until lightly browned on all sides and the chicken is opaque throughout, 7–10 minutes. Transfer to a platter and serve at once with the dipping sauce (following).

Mango Dipping Sauce

● In a bowl, combine the onion and oil and let soak until the onion has softened, about 10 minutes. Transfer the onion mixture to a nonreactive saucepan, add the mangoes, orange juice, garlic, lime juice, and honey, and stir to mix. Place over medium-high heat and cook, stirring occasionally, until the mangoes are soft and the flavors are blended, about 15 minutes. Remove from the heat and let cool.

● Transfer the sauce to a blender and purée to the desired consistency. You should have about 2 cups (16 fl oz/500 ml). (The dipping sauce can be covered and refrigerated for up to 1 day before serving.) To serve, divide the dipping sauce among small cups or bowls and place alongside the kebabs.

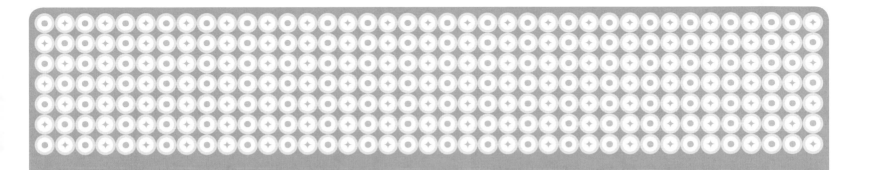

halloween P·A·R·T·Y

Ghosts, goblins, and black cats of all ages will have a blast at this spooky gathering. Play up the holiday's theme with decorations in black and orange, a costume chest, and finger foods fit for witches. Kids entertain themselves with dressing up, bobbing for apples, and helping to make their own trick-or-treat goody bags.

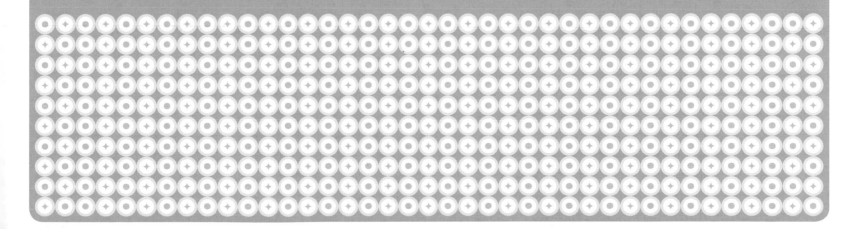

party style

invitations Send or hand out invites that match the theme. Cut out Halloween-inspired shapes, such as pumpkins or witches' hats, from orange construction paper, and write the message with a glitter pen. Or, use black masquerade masks, which kids can then wear.

decorations and favors Weave the holiday's colors and spooky themes into the décor: black and orange paper chains, a white, gauzy table covering, cobwebs over the windows, and spiders and skeletons everywhere.

food To balance the sweets, serve an array of savory treats that are fun to eat, like celery with peanut butter and raisins (ants on a log), halved hard-boiled eggs with sliced olives (eyeball eggs), and cheesy bread sticks.

Take-Home Draculas Wrap extra popcorn balls in black tissue paper and attach eyes and fangs for creepy (and delicious!) takeaways.

Party Beacons Include freaky harbingers of things to come in the invitations, such as witches' fingers and spiders. A paper-covered matchbox makes a nice kid-sized container.

Jack-o'-Lantern Plates Layer orange and black paper plates, cut a face through the top layer with an X-Acto knife, and watch the jack-o'-lantern appear.

Creepy Crawly Décor Spread a piece of gauze fabric (found at craft or Halloween stores) over the serving table. Add spiders, rats, bugs, and a mummy's hand for frightening appeal.

"Dirty" Popcorn Balls Sticky popcorn balls slithering with gummi worms and rolled in cookie-crumb dirt are gooey snacks kids can make themselves.

Healthy Snacks Include some fresh and savory Halloween treats, such as hard-boiled eggs, raisin-studded peanut butter in celery, and cucumber or carrot sticks, along with the sweets.

Spidery Ice Cubes Creepy black spiders imprisoned in cubes of ice and colorful straws crawling with ants add intrigue to any fright-night beverage.

Halloween Cookies For a spooky treat, use Decorating Icing (page 134) to dress up Sugar Cookies (page 140) with holiday symbols and colors. Try ghosts, black cats, pumpkins, witches, spiders, or bats.

party plan

overall strategy Decoration is key to a great Halloween party. Make sure to leave yourself plenty of time to experiment with all kinds of spooky décor, then think about what to serve and play.

what to serve Halloween sweets are always fun, but balance them out with some healthier offerings. Try grilled cheese sandwiches shaped with cookie cutters into ghosts or pumpkins, slices of pumpkin bread, and dressed-up crudités (page 88).

serving suggestions Spiderwebs, crawly bugs, witches' fingers, rats, and snakes can all make their way onto plates and platters laden with treats.

recipes

Blood-Red Punch

○●○

Caramel Apples

○●○

"Dirty" Popcorn Balls

○●○

Pumpkin Bread

ahead of time

parents
- Make the punch, pumpkin bread, and spider-infested ice cubes, and assemble a healthy snack or two.
- Help kids with the decorations and with making the caramel apples.
- Music will help set the mood. Look for a Halloween CD at a party store or department store, or make your own playlist.
- Ready the trick-or-treat bags.

kids
- Help with the caramel apples and cookies.
- Begin working on the decorations!

day of the party

parents
- Arrange separate stations around the party room for games and activities.
- Decorate the serving table, plates, and platters.
- Pop the popcorn for the balls.
- Arrange snacks and spooky treats on serving tables and trays.

kids
- Help decorate the table.

during the party

parents
- Assist kids with games and other activities.

kids
- Make the popcorn balls.
- Don a costume and have fun.
- Trick-or-treat!

activity ideas

Scary Treats Decorate sugar cookies with a Halloween theme, pick from a cauldron of trick-or-treat candies, or roll "worm-infested" sticky popcorn balls in cookie "dirt" for deliciously disgusting treats.

Witches' Brew Begin with a simple black cauldron. Fill it with water and apples for bobbing, or with oiled cooked spaghetti and prizes for a blindfolded game of guess what's in the witches' brew.

Costume Contest No Halloween party is complete without costumes. Stage a parade and take a lot of pictures!

Blood-Red Punch

In a 2-qt (2-l) pitcher or punch bowl, combine the juice, sparkling water, puréed berries, and ice. Stir gently to mix. Divide the punch evenly among 8 glasses.

Scary Ice Cubes Place Halloween items (such as plastic spiders and bugs or gummi worms) in ice-cube trays, leaving a little of each item exposed. (Be sure each item is big enough not to be easily swallowed.) Fill the tray with water and freeze. Place several cubes in each glass before filling with punch.

Caramel Apples

In a small saucepan over medium heat, combine the caramels and water. Heat, stirring occasionally, until smooth, 5–7 minutes. Keep warm over low heat.

Insert a Popsicle stick or lollipop stick into the stem end of each apple. Line a baking sheet with waxed paper. Dip an apple into the caramel, coating it completely and letting the excess drip back into the pan, and place on the waxed paper. Repeat with the remaining apples, using a spoon to scoop caramel onto the sides of the apples. Let stand on the prepared baking sheet until the caramel has set, about 10 minutes.

Eat immediately, or wrap individually in waxed paper and store in the refrigerator for up to 1 day. Bring to room temperature before serving.

Chocolate-Dipped Variation Put 1 cup (6 oz/185 g) semisweet (plain) chocolate chips into a heatproof bowl and place over (not touching) barely simmering water in a saucepan. Heat, stirring occasionally, until melted and smooth, about 5 minutes. Dip each apple in the caramel as directed, letting the excess drip off, and then into the chocolate, coating only the bottom half. Or, drizzle the chocolate over the apple, letting it drip down the sides.

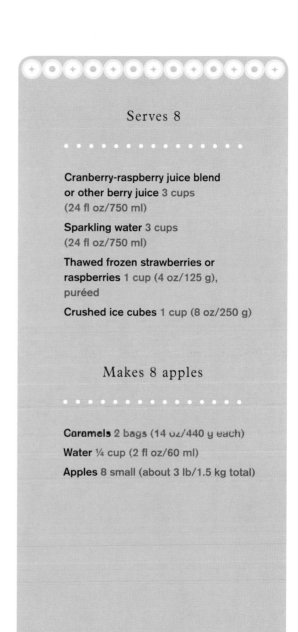

Serves 8

Cranberry-raspberry juice blend or other berry juice 3 cups (24 fl oz/750 ml)

Sparkling water 3 cups (24 fl oz/750 ml)

Thawed frozen strawberries or raspberries 1 cup (4 oz/125 g), puréed

Crushed ice cubes 1 cup (8 oz/250 g)

Makes 8 apples

Caramels 2 bags (14 oz/440 g each)

Water ¼ cup (2 fl oz/60 ml)

Apples 8 small (about 3 lb/1.5 kg total)

You can prepare these dressed-up popcorn balls in advance, or let the kids make them during the party. If using microwave popcorn for these treats, choose a low-salt or salt-free variety.

"Dirty" Popcorn Balls

Makes 8 balls

· · · · · · · · · · · · · · · · ·

Popped corn 12 cups (one 6-oz/185-g package microwave popcorn)

Unsalted butter 4 tablespoons

Miniature marshmallows 4½ cups (8 oz/225 g)

Chocolate cookie crumbs ½ cup (1 oz/30 g)

Unsweetened cocoa powder 4 teaspoons

Gummi worms 16 (about 6 oz/185 g)

● Pour the popcorn into a large bowl. Set aside.

● In a large microwave-safe bowl, microwave the butter on High until melted, about 45 seconds. Add the marshmallows and stir to coat. Microwave on High until the marshmallows start to melt and look puffy, about 1½ minutes. Meanwhile, in a shallow bowl, combine the cookie crumbs and cocoa powder. Toss to mix.

● Stir together the melted marshmallows and butter until smooth. Pour the warm marshmallow mixture over the popcorn and stir to coat the popcorn evenly.

● Using well-buttered hands, scoop up a handful of the popcorn and shape into a baseball-sized ball, pressing firmly. Pull apart 2 openings in the ball and place the worms inside, letting their heads and some parts of their bodies peek through. Close the ball and press firmly to seal the worms inside. Roll the balls in the cookie-crumb mixture until roughly coated.

● Eat at once, or wrap in waxed paper or plastic wrap and store at room temperature for up to 2 days.

Preparation Tip To mash the cookies for the "dirt," place whole chocolate cookies in a sturdy lock-top plastic bag and press them with the back of a spoon.

Candy Corn Variation Skip the cookie crumbs and gummi worms. Tint the melted marshmallow mixture with orange food coloring. Mix a big handful of candy corn into the popcorn with the marshmallow mixture and form into balls as directed.

This recipe makes 2 loaves, which should leave you with a few extra slices after the guests have gone. You can make them up to 4 days in advance and store them, well wrapped, at room temperature.

Pumpkin Bread

⬤ Preheat the oven to 350°F (180°C). Butter two 9-by-5-inch (23-by-13-cm) loaf pans, then dust with flour, tapping out the excess. Set aside.

⬤ In a bowl, stir together the flour, baking soda, salt, baking powder, cinnamon, cloves, and nutmeg. Set aside. In a large bowl, combine the pumpkin, sugar, oil, eggs, and vanilla and stir until well mixed. Stir in the flour mixture just until blended.

⬤ Divide the batter evenly between the prepared pans. If desired, sprinkle the nuts evenly over the tops.

⬤ Bake until the tops are lightly browned and a toothpick inserted into the center of each loaf comes out clean, 50–55 minutes. Let the loaves cool in the pans on wire racks for 10 minutes, Then turn the loaves out onto the racks, turn the loaves upright, and let cool completely. Cut into 1-inch-thick slices to serve.

Serving Suggestion Drizzle the loaves with Decorating Icing (page 134) and nuts, then top with black plastic spiders.

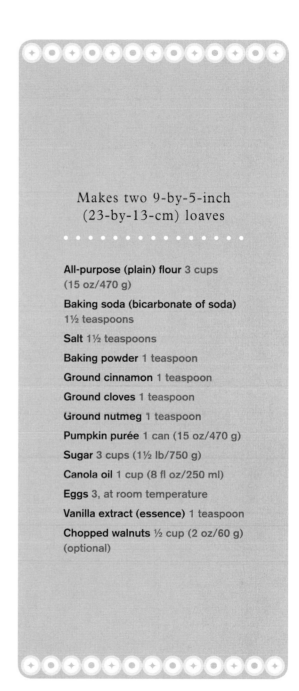

Makes two 9-by-5-inch
(23-by-13-cm) loaves

All-purpose (plain) flour 3 cups
(15 oz/470 g)

Baking soda (bicarbonate of soda)
1½ teaspoons

Salt 1½ teaspoons

Baking powder 1 teaspoon

Ground cinnamon 1 teaspoon

Ground cloves 1 teaspoon

Ground nutmeg 1 teaspoon

Pumpkin purée 1 can (15 oz/470 g)

Sugar 3 cups (1½ lb/750 g)

Canola oil 1 cup (8 fl oz/250 ml)

Eggs 3, at room temperature

Vanilla extract (essence) 1 teaspoon

Chopped walnuts ½ cup (2 oz/60 g)
(optional)

pizza P·A·R·T·Y

Pizza is one subject most kids know a lot about. Provide them with individual rounds of dough and a selection of toppings, then watch as each kid becomes a master pizza chef. Have a contest for the pizza with the funniest face—using shredded zucchini for hair, olives for eyes, and pepper rings for mouths—then display the edible creations for all to see.

party style

invitations Focus on invitations that introduce party activities. Print on disks of yellow paper and decorate with pizza-topping confetti, or on iron-on transfer paper for applying to aprons or cloth napkins.

decorations and favors Focus on any hobbies the young host or hostess might share with guests. Sports are often popular with boys, as are all types of vehicles and dinosaurs and other prehistoric creatures.

food Pizza will dominate the menu. Partner it with a crisp green salad, a few healthy snacks (bowls of peanuts in the shell and orange slices contribute to the sports theme), and maybe cupcakes, and the kids will have a meal that will last them through the day.

Party Favor Pails Kids can't wait to dig into festive striped tin pails brimming with sporty treats, like chocolate baseballs, soccer balls, and basketballs.

Champion Cupcakes These mini-cakes can be customized to suit any type of party. Green jimmies and tinted frosting create a believable playing field for tiny sports figures.

Pizza Places White easel or butcher paper is an ideal table covering for messy pizza meals—and is a good way for kids to find their places.

Streamers Thick, colorful strips of crêpe paper or streamers offer numerous decorating options. Try them over windows and doorways, as a table skirt, or strung from the ceiling.

Friendly Competition Pizza making becomes a sports event when the creative use of vegetables lends itself to a face-making contest. Display the winning trio on numbered pedestals.

Medal Themes Award pizza chefs with chocolate-coin "medals" and stacks of baseball cards. Water bottles get star treatment with ribboned nameplates.

party plan

overall strategy Make the dough and sauce well ahead, and assemble toppings and side dishes the day of the party. Kids add toppings to pizza rounds at the party, then bake and eat their pies within minutes.

what to serve Offer fresh, healthy accompaniments that balance the rich flavor of the pizzas. A crisp green salad, crunchy crudités, orange sections, apple slices, or whole strawberries are good choices.

serving suggestions Suggesting themes or contests for pizza making encourages kids to be more adventurous in their topping choices. For serving, use paper plates and napkins. Italian cheeses can be salty, so make sure to have plenty of beverages on hand, such as sparkling water or fruity Italian sodas.

recipes

Pizza Dough

Quick Tomato Sauce

Chopped Green Salad

ahead of time

parents
- Make the sauce.
- Make the dough.
- Assemble the goody bags or buckets, and any game prizes.
- Make the cupcakes or other party dessert.

kids
- Help come up with games and prizes.

day of the party

parents
- Clear a large workstation in the kitchen where kids can make their pizzas.
- Leave the pizza dough at room temperature for 1½ hours before making the pizzas.
- Assemble all the pizza toppings (including the tomato sauce and shredded cheese) in separate bowls. Cover until ready to use.
- Make the salad or other accompaniments.

kids
- Shred the cheese, and cut up meats and vegetables for the toppings.

during the party

parents
- Divide the pizza dough into 12 equal pieces. If the kids are especially young, shape the pieces into 7-inch (18-cm) rounds.
- Bake the finished pizzas.

kids
- Shape the pizza crusts and top them.
- Play games, eat, and have fun!

activity ideas

Trading Cards Whether it's baseball or Pokémon, kids love a good set of trading cards. Offer them as prizes or in goody pails, with plenty of time left over for trading.

Popcorn Prize Bucket A large container filled with popcorn can hide lots of tiny prizes. Blindfold the kids and let them each dig into the bucket to seek out 2 or 3 items for their goody pail before it's the next kid's turn.

Pizza-Making Contest Nothing inspires creative use of ingredients better than a contest. Try a face-making competition, with chocolate coins on ribbons for the "medals."

Outdoor Play If the weather is nice, take the sports theme into the backyard for some outdoor playtime. Have on hand the sports equipment featured on the cupcakes, party pails, and other decorations. Try a soccer-ball cone course, hoops in kid-height baskets, or a game of Wiffle ball.

making pizzas

Pizza dough is easier to make than you might think, especially if you use a stand mixer for mixing and kneading. It is also a perfect make-ahead recipe, as the dough can be refrigerated for up to 12 hours, or frozen for up to 2 months. (For recipe and make-ahead instructions, see page 108.)

The recipe makes enough for 12 kid-sized pizzas. For the party, give each kid a piece of dough (or form the dough rounds yourself), and set out the sauce, cheese, and a good range of toppings. Use 2 ovens to bake the pizzas, or bake them in shifts if necessary.

creative ideas and tips

- Mozzarella cheese is the most popular pizza cheese, but you can offer plenty of other good melting cheeses too, such as Monterey jack, Swiss, Fontina, a young Asiago, or a mild Cheddar. Plan on a total of about 2 lb (1 kg).

- Provide sliced vegetables in every variety, such as bell peppers (capsicums), zucchini (courgettes), mushrooms, and olives. Corn kernels, broccoli florets, spinach leaves, and halved cherry tomatoes are all delicious.

- Offer sliced cooked sausages, diced cooked chicken or ham, crisped bacon strips, and/or sliced pepperoni or salami.

- Without some type of incentive, most kids will play it safe and top their pizzas with only a splash of sauce and a sprinkling of cheese. But give them a goal to shoot for—such as a prize for the funniest face created with the toppings—and junior Picassos are born. Best of all, you'll have them eating more vegetables than you ever thought possible.

You can make this dough in advance of the party day, then refrigerate or freeze it. Bring to room temperature before using, about 1½ hours for refrigerated dough, or 6 hours for frozen.

**Makes enough for
12 small pizzas**

Pizza Dough

DOUGH

Lukewarm water about 110°F/43°C
3 cups (24 fl oz/750 ml)

Active dry yeast 2 packages
(2½ teaspoons each)

Salt 1 teaspoon

Olive oil 2 tablespoons, plus more
for oiling bowl

All-purpose (plain) flour about 8 cups
(2½ lb/1.2 kg)

Cornmeal for pans

Quick Tomato Sauce 1 recipe
(opposite)

Assorted toppings (page 107)

To make the dough, in the bowl of a stand mixer fitted with the paddle attachment, sprinkle the yeast on top of the water and let stand until foamy, about 5 minutes. Add the salt, oil, and 5 cups (25 oz/780 g) of the flour and beat on medium speed until the dough is glossy and stretchy, about 5 minutes. On low speed, beat in 2½ cups (12½ oz/390 g) more of the flour until combined.

If you have a dough hook, attach it to the mixer and beat the dough on medium speed, gradually adding up to ¼ cup (1½ oz/45 g) more flour if needed, until it is springy and pulls cleanly away from the sides of the bowl, 5–7 minutes. If you don't have a dough hook, turn out the dough onto a well-floured surface and knead until smooth and springy, 10–15 minutes, adding as little additional flour as possible to prevent sticking.

Oil a large bowl, place the dough in the bowl, and turn to oil the top. Cover with plastic wrap and let rise in a warm place until doubled in bulk, about 45 minutes, or in the refrigerator for up to 12 hours. (To freeze, let dough rise, punch down, seal in a lock-top plastic bag, and freeze for up to 2 months; bring to room temperature before continuing.)

Position racks in the lower third and middle of 2 ovens and preheat to 425°F (220°C) (or bake in batches if only 1 oven is available). Lightly sprinkle 4 baking sheets with cornmeal. Punch down the dough, turn out onto a floured surface, and press flat to release excess air. If the dough has risen in the refrigerator, cover with a kitchen towel and bring to room temperature before continuing. Cut the dough into 12 equal portions.

Help kids press and stretch dough into rounds (don't work it too much or it won't stretch) about 7 inches (18 cm) in diameter. Instruct them to top each round with a spoonful of sauce, a sprinkling of cheese, and desired toppings. Place 3 rounds on each prepared pan and bake until the crust is golden and the cheese is bubbly, 12–15 minutes. Let cool slightly before serving.

This classic tomato sauce cooks in a jiffy with no sacrifice to flavor. Use one large spoonful on each kid-sized pizza. If freshly made, refrigerate any leftovers for 3 days or freeze for up to 1 month.

Quick Tomato Sauce

● In a large saucepan over medium heat, warm the oil. Add the onion and sauté, stirring occasionally, until tender and translucent, about 10 minutes. Add the garlic and sauté for 1 minute longer. Add the tomatoes, tomato paste, and oregano, stirring to combine. Raise the heat to medium-high and cook, stirring occasionally to break up the tomatoes, until the excess moisture evaporates and the sauce is a good spreading consistency, 10–15 minutes. (The sauce can be cooled, covered, and refrigerated for up to 3 days before using.)

● Season to taste with salt and pepper. Let cool to lukewarm before spreading on the dough rounds.

Makes about 2½ cups (20 fl oz/625 ml)

Olive oil 1 tablespoon

Yellow onion ¼, finely chopped

Garlic 1 clove, minced

Diced tomatoes 1 can (28 oz/875 g), drained

Tomato paste 1 tablespoon

Oregano or basil 2 teaspoons fresh minced or ½ teaspoon dried

Salt and freshly ground pepper

CREAMY GARLIC DRESSING

Light mayonnaise ¾ cup
(6 fl oz/180 ml)

Water 3 tablespoons

Whole milk 1 tablespoon

White wine vinegar 2½ teaspoons

Garlic 1 clove, finely minced

Sugar ½ teaspoon

Salt ¼ teaspoon

SALAD

Romaine (cos) lettuce 1 heart

Iceberg lettuce ⅓ head

Celery 6 stalks, diced

English (hothouse) cucumbers 3,
peeled, halved, seeded, and diced

Avocados 2, pitted, peeled, and
diced (optional)

Garlic croutons 2 cups (4 oz/125 g)

Kids love this crisp green salad for its simplicity and its mild and creamy garlic dressing. If you decide to include the avocados, make sure you add them just before serving so they are at their best.

Chopped Green Salad

To make the dressing, in a small bowl or jar, combine the mayonnaise, water, milk, vinegar, garlic, sugar, and salt. Mix with a fork until blended. Set aside.

To make the salad, cut the romaine leaves lengthwise into strips ¾ inch (2 cm) wide, then cut crosswise into rough squares. Place in a large salad bowl. Cut the iceberg lettuce into slices ¾ inch (2 cm) thick, then cut crosswise into rough cubes. Add the celery and cucumbers. (At this point, the salad can be covered and refrigerated for up to 8 hours.)

Just before serving, add the avocados, if desired. Sprinkle the croutons over the salad, drizzle the dressing over the top, and toss gently to mix. Or, toss the salad without the dressing, divide among individual bowls, and drizzle the dressing on top. Serve at once.

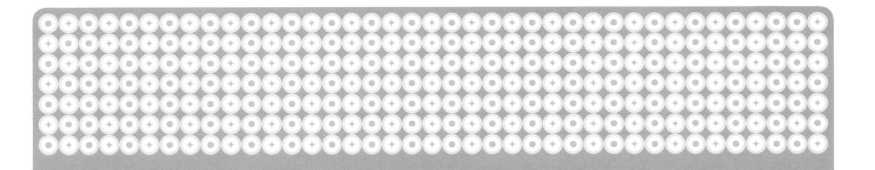

winter P·A·R·T·Y

Celebrate the chilliest time of the year with a heartwarming menu and a flurry of cold-weather activities. Whether the ground outside is bone-dry or buried under a blanket of snow, a blizzard will be raging indoors. Decorate with a storm of lacy snowflakes, which the kids can help make. Kids ages 5 and up will have the most fun with the fondue.

party style

invitations Paper snowflake cutouts pasted onto colorful craft-paper cards make lovely invitations, as do penguins, snowmen, and other winter icons. You might add sleds, skates, or skis, if the party includes them.

decorations and favors Think snow. A flurry of snowflakes drifting overhead, nestled onto napkins, or swooping over chair backs lend the sensation of an indoor blizzard. Icy blue accents reinforce the theme.

food Hot cheese and chocolate fondues and steaming mugs of cider and cocoa warm chilly kids right down to their fingertips. For a wintry birthday celebration, make snow-crystal cupcakes (use rock-candy chunks) or a cake with all-white decorations.

Paper Snowflakes These pretty cutouts can adorn all kinds of party treats and decorations. Use them to make a festive ring for a noise blower, a delicate garland, and a magical mobile.

Hot Spiced Cider For extra spicy flavor, rub the mug rim with the cut edge of an apple or lemon wedge, then dip in cinnamon sugar.

Snow Globes Use a glue gun to affix tiny figures onto a jar lid. Fill the jar with distilled water and a spoonful of glycerin. Add sparkly glitter for snow. Rim the lid with silicone sealant and screw on tight.

Hot Cocoa To make it extra minty, coat the rim with crushed peppermint candies and add a candy cane straw.

Surprising Place Cards Individual snowflake garlands, each printed with a guest's name, make a good substitute for traditional place cards and double as unique take-home party favors.

Fluffy Party Hats Like the icy fluff of a snowball, fun curled-ribbon pom-poms make ordinary party hats look like the caps of wintertime elves.

Snowflake Cakes Use the filigree edge of saucer-sized white doilies to make collars for cupcakes. Top with blue-tinted icing and shredded coconut or sugar crystals for a distinctive icy finish.

Chocolate Fondue Tasty partners for chocolate are easy to find. Serve pound or angel food cake, marshmallows, and a variety of fresh and dried fruits.

party plan

overall strategy Save time by making less perishable items, such as the cider and chocolate fondue, well ahead of time, then make the snugglers and cheese fondue just before the guests arrive.

what to serve Try lightly steamed broccoli florets with the cheese fondue as a healthy alternative to bread, and a variety of fresh and dried fruits with the chocolate. On a snowy day, give each kid a cup and a choice of juices or flavored syrups to make snow cones.

serving suggestions Rim drink mugs with crushed peppermint candies or cinnamon sugar. Place dippers in sparkly glass bowls or on platters lined with doilies.

recipes

Hot Spiced Cider

Snugglers

Cheese Fondue

Chocolate Fondue

ahead of time

parents
- Make the cider.
- Make the chocolate fondue.
- Plan for party games and items for making snow globes or other cold-weather crafts.

kids
- Shred the cheese for the fondue.
- Cut out paper snowflakes for decorating.

day of the party

parents
- Cut up French bread, fruit, and cake for the fondues, then arrange on platters.
- Reheat the cider and ready it for serving when guests arrive.
- Make the snugglers.
- Make the cheese fondue just before the party begins. Keep warm, stirring occasionally, until ready to serve.

kids
- Help parents decorate.

during the party

parents
- Offer guests cocoa or cider as they arrive.
- Set up the cheese (then the chocolate) fondue in an easily accessible spot. Keep warm over Sterno or other heat source.
- Reheat the chocolate fondue just before serving.

kids
- Make wintry crafts and play games.
- If there's snow, enjoy it with sleds and skates, or make snow cones with syrup.

activity ideas

Snowball Catchall Scooping a spoonful of cotton balls into a bowl while blindfolded is more difficult than you might think. The kid with the most cottonballs after 3 scoops wins.

Pin the Nose on the Snowman For this wintry rendition of the popular party game, make a large snowman from paper, and use orange pom-pom noses set with double-sided tape.

Snowflakes Fold white paper circles into eighths, cut small holes from all sides, and open to reveal a snowflake.

Hot Spiced Cider

◉ In a large pot, combine the apple juice, brown sugar, cinnamon sticks, nutmeg, and allspice. Pierce the orange peel with the cloves and add to the pot. Bring just to a boil over medium-high heat, reduce the heat to low, and simmer for 10 minutes.

◉ Divide the cider evenly among 8 mugs. Garnish each with a cinnamon stick. Serve hot.

Serving Suggestions To coat the rim of each mug with cinnamon sugar before filling, rub the cut edge of an apple wedge along the rim, and then dip the rim into a saucer of cinnamon sugar. Or, garnish each mug with a twist of orange peel.

Snugglers

◉ In a saucepan over medium heat, warm the milk until small bubbles appear around the edges of the pan. Meanwhile, in a small bowl or cup, stir together the cocoa powder and the sugar, breaking up any lumps, then stir in the peppermint extract. Add about ¼ cup (2 fl oz/60 ml) of the milk to the cocoa powder mixture and stir until blended.

◉ Just before serving, stir the chocolate mixture into the hot milk. Divide the cocoa evenly among 8 mugs. Serve hot.

Topping Suggestions Garnish each serving with a sprinkling of miniature marshmallows and a peppermint-stick straw, or with a dollop of lightly sweetened whipped cream and a sprinkling of crushed peppermint candies. To coat the rim of each mug with crushed peppermint candies before filling, brush the rim with simple syrup (1 part sugar dissolved in 1 part boiling water), and then dip the rim into a saucer of crushed candies.

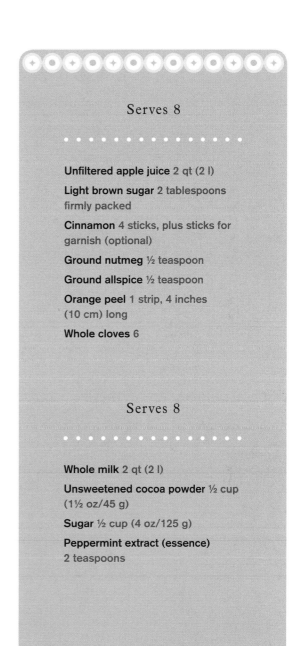

Serves 8

Unfiltered apple juice 2 qt (2 l)

Light brown sugar 2 tablespoons firmly packed

Cinnamon 4 sticks, plus sticks for garnish (optional)

Ground nutmeg ½ teaspoon

Ground allspice ½ teaspoon

Orange peel 1 strip, 4 inches (10 cm) long

Whole cloves 6

Serves 8

Whole milk 2 qt (2 l)

Unsweetened cocoa powder ½ cup (1½ oz/45 g)

Sugar ½ cup (4 oz/125 g)

Peppermint extract (essence) 2 teaspoons

If your fondue pot can't take medium-high heat on the stove top,

make this kid-friendly fondue—broth replaces the traditional

wine—in a saucepan and transfer it to the fondue pot for serving.

Serves 8

. . . .

Gruyère cheese 2 cups (8 oz/250 g) shredded

Emmentaler, Swiss, or Fontina cheese 2 cups (8 oz/250 g) shredded

Cornstarch (cornflour) 2 tablespoons

Garlic ½ clove

Vegetable broth ½ cup (4 fl oz/125 ml)

Water ½ cup (4 fl oz/125 ml)

Cider vinegar 3 tablespoons

French bread 1 or 2 loaves, cut into 1-inch (2.5-cm) pieces

Cheese Fondue

● Place the Gruyère and Emmentaler cheeses in a lock-top plastic bag, add the cornstarch, seal closed, and shake until the cheeses are evenly coated. Rub the cut side of the garlic clove around the inside of the fondue pot; discard the garlic.

● Pour the vegetable broth, water, and cider vinegar into the fondue pot. Place the pot over medium-high heat and bring just to a boil. Reduce the heat to medium and whisk a handful of the cheese mixture into the broth mixture until it is almost melted. Repeat with the remaining cheese mixture in about 4 batches. Continue whisking until the cheese is completely melted and the fondue bubbles, about 1 minute longer.

● Set the pot over Sterno or other heat source to keep warm. Put the bread in a basket and place alongside the pot. Outfit the kids with fondue forks and serve.

Dipper Suggestions Set out apple wedges and lightly steamed broccoli florets with the bread cubes.

Troubleshooting Tip If the fondue separates during cooking, remove the clump of solid cheese from the pot and chop into small pieces. Whisk an additional 1 teaspoon cornstarch into the hot broth mixture remaining in the pot and stir over medium-high heat until slightly thickened. Then return the chopped cheese to the broth mixture and whisk until smooth.

This is a great make-ahead dessert—prepare the fondue a day or two in advance, then let cool, cover, and refrigerate. Reheat, stirring occasionally, over medium heat while you assemble the dippers.

Chocolate Fondue

In a small saucepan over medium-low heat, combine the chocolate chips, cream, and corn syrup. Heat, stirring occasionally, until melted and smooth, 8–10 minutes.

Transfer the chocolate mixture to a fondue pot and set the pot over Sterno or other heat source to keep warm. Put the dippers on plates or platters alongside. Outfit the kids with fondue forks and serve.

White Chocolate Variation Substitute white chocolate chips for the semisweet chocolate chips.

Dipper Suggestions Use whole strawberries, thick banana slices, pineapple chunks, orange wedges, marshmallows, and/or cubes of pound cake or angel food cake.

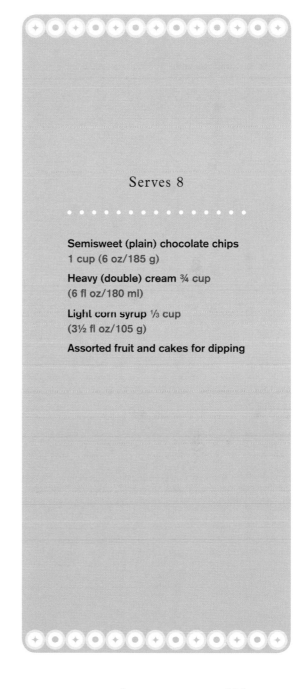

Serves 8

Semisweet (plain) chocolate chips
1 cup (6 oz/185 g)

Heavy (double) cream ¾ cup
(6 fl oz/180 ml)

Light corn syrup ⅓ cup
(3½ fl oz/105 g)

Assorted fruit and cakes for dipping

birthday recipes

No birthday party is complete without a special sweet treat (or two) crafted especially for the celebrant. Use the following recipes for cakes, cookies, and ice creams as the building blocks for making party-perfect desserts. And remember, when it's time to decorate—and to personalize your sweet creation for the birthday kid—the sky is the limit.

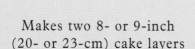

This classic cake is a cinch to make from scratch. Let the butter, eggs, and milk come to room temperature before mixing, and the batter will blend more smoothly, resulting in a delicate texture.

Makes two 8- or 9-inch
(20- or 23-cm) cake layers

· · · · · · · · · · · · · · · · · · ·

All-purpose (plain) flour 2¼ cups
(11½ oz/360 g)

Baking powder 1 tablespoon

Salt ¼ teaspoon

Unsalted butter ¾ cup (6 oz/185 g),
at room temperature

Sugar 1¾ cups (14 oz/440 g)

Vanilla extract (essence) 2 teaspoons

Large eggs 3, at room temperature

Whole milk 1⅓ cups (11 fl oz/340 ml),
at room temperature

Vanilla Cake

● Preheat the oven to 350°F (180°C). Butter two 8- or 9-inch (20- or 23-cm) round cake pans and dust with flour, tapping out the excess.

● In a bowl, stir together the flour, baking powder, and salt. Set aside.

● In a large bowl, using a handheld mixer or a stand mixer fitted with the paddle attachment, beat together the butter, sugar, and vanilla on medium speed until creamy, about 3 minutes. Add the eggs, one at a time, beating well after each addition. Turn off the mixer and scrape down the sides of the bowl with a rubber spatula. With the mixer on low speed, add the flour mixture in 3 additions alternately with the milk mixture in 2 additions, beginning and ending with the flour mixture and beating just until blended after each addition. Scrape down the bowl with the spatula.

● Pour the batter into the prepared pans, dividing it evenly. Bake until golden and a toothpick inserted into the center of each cake comes out clean, 30–35 minutes. Transfer the cakes to wire racks and let cool in the pans for 20 minutes. Then invert onto plates, lift off the pans, and invert again onto the racks. Let cool completely.

Make-Ahead Tip The cake layers can be baked up to 2 days in advance, well wrapped in plastic wrap, and stored at room temperature.

Rich and moist, this easy-to-make chocolate cake will put a smile on any kid's face. As with the Vanilla Cake (opposite), have all of the ingredients at room temperature for smooth mixing.

Chocolate Cake

⊕ Preheat the oven to 350°F (180°C). Butter two 9-inch (23-cm) round cake pans. Line the cake pans with parchment (baking) paper, cut to fit the pans exactly. Butter the paper and then sprinkle lightly with flour, tapping out the excess.

⊕ Place the chocolate in a heatproof bowl and set over (not touching) simmering water in a saucepan. Heat, stirring often, until melted and smooth, about 5 minutes. Set aside.

⊕ In a bowl, stir together the flour, baking soda, and salt. Set aside.

⊕ In a large bowl, using a handheld mixer or a stand mixer fitted with the paddle attachment, beat together the butter and sugars on medium speed until creamy, about 2 minutes. Add the eggs, one at a time, beating well after each addition. Turn off the mixer and scrape down the sides of the bowl with a rubber spatula. Add the vanilla and beat for 1 minute longer. Add the melted chocolate and beat until evenly blended. With the mixer on low speed, add the flour mixture in 3 additions alternately with the buttermilk in 2 additions, beginning and ending with the flour mixture and beating just until blended after each addition. Scrape down the bowl with the spatula.

⊕ Pour the batter into the prepared pans, dividing it evenly. Bake until a toothpick inserted into the center of each cake comes out clean, 30–35 minutes. Transfer the cakes to wire racks and let cool in the pans for 20 minutes. Then invert onto plates, lift off the pans, peel off the parchment paper, and invert again onto the racks. Let cool completely.

Make-Ahead Tip The cake layers can be baked up to 1 day in advance, well wrapped in plastic wrap, and stored at room temperature.

Makes two 9-inch (23-cm) cake layers

Unsweetened chocolate 4 oz (125 g), finely chopped

All-purpose (plain) flour 2¼ cups (11½ oz/360 g)

Baking soda 1 teaspoon

Salt ¼ teaspoon

Unsalted butter 1 cup (8 oz/250 g), at room temperature

Light brown sugar 1 cup (7 oz/220 g), firmly packed

Granulated sugar ¾ cup (6 oz/185 g)

Large eggs 4, at room temperature

Vanilla extract (essence) 2 teaspoons

Low-fat or nonfat buttermilk 1 cup (8 fl oz/250 ml), at room temperature

Kids will go nuts for this triple-color cake. It can be well wrapped and stored at room temperature for up to 2 days before serving. Top with Dark Chocolate Glaze (page 133) or tinted fondant (page 17).

Makes one 9-inch (23-cm) cake

· · · · · · · · · · · · · · · · · · ·

All-purpose (plain) flour 2¼ cups (11½ oz/360 g)

Baking powder 1 tablespoon

Salt ¼ teaspoon

Unsalted butter ½ cup (4 oz/125 g) plus 2 tablespoons, at room temperature

Sugar 1¾ cups (14 oz/440 g)

Vanilla extract (essence) 1 teaspoon

Large eggs 3, at room temperature

Whole milk 1¼ cups (10 fl oz/310 ml), at room temperature

Unsweetened cocoa powder 2 tablespoons

Very hot water 2 tablespoons

Raspberry extract (essence) ⅛ teaspoon

Red food coloring 4 or 5 drops

Marble Cake

Preheat the oven to 350°F (180°C). Butter a 9-inch (23-cm) springform pan with 2-inch (5-cm) sides. Line the pan with parchment (baking) paper, cut to fit exactly. Butter the paper and then sprinkle lightly with flour, tapping out the excess.

For the vanilla batter, in a bowl, stir together the flour, baking powder, and salt; set aside. In a large bowl, using a handheld mixer or a stand mixer fitted with the paddle attachment, beat together the butter, sugar, and vanilla on medium speed until creamy, about 3 minutes. Add the eggs, one at a time, beating well after each addition. Turn off the mixer and scrape down the sides of the bowl with a rubber spatula. With the mixer on low speed, beat in the flour mixture in 3 additions alternately with the milk in 2 additions, beginning and ending with the flour mixture and beating just until blended after each addition. Scrape down the bowl with the spatula.

For the chocolate batter, in a small bowl, combine the cocoa powder and hot water and stir until smooth. Add 1 cup (8 fl oz/250 ml) of the vanilla batter and stir until blended. For the raspberry batter, in a small bowl, stir together ½ cup (4 fl oz/125 ml) of the vanilla batter, the raspberry extract, and the red food coloring until blended.

Pour the remaining vanilla batter into the prepared cake pan, spreading it evenly. Add the chocolate batter in big globs over the vanilla, then drizzle the raspberry batter over the top. Draw the tip of a kitchen knife through the batter, making several swirls and gently pushing all the way through to the bottom of the pan.

Bake until golden and a toothpick inserted into the center of the cake comes out clean, 45–50 minutes. Transfer to a wire rack and let cool in the pan for 10 minutes. Remove the pan sides, invert the cake onto a rack, remove the bottom, peel off the parchment, and invert again onto the rack. Let cool completely.

This light-textured cake, the perfect centerpiece for warm-weather parties, is delicious with Vanilla Frosting (page 132) or Cream Cheese Frosting (page 50). Or, use the citrusy batter for making cupcakes.

Lemon Cake

● Preheat the oven to 350°F (180°C). Butter two 8- or 9-inch (20- or 23-cm) round cake pans and dust with flour, tapping out the excess.

● In a bowl, stir together the flour, baking powder, and salt. Set aside.

● In a large bowl, using a handheld mixer or a stand mixer fitted with the paddle attachment, beat together the butter, sugar, vanilla, lemon extract, and lemon zest on medium speed until creamy, about 3 minutes. Add the eggs, one at a time, beating well after each addition. Turn off the mixer and scrape down the sides of the bowl with a rubber spatula. With the mixer on low speed, beat in the flour mixture in 3 additions alternately with the milk in 2 additions, beginning and ending with the flour mixture and beating just until blended after each addition. Scrape down the bowl with the rubber spatula.

● Pour the batter into the prepared pans, dividing it evenly. Bake until golden and a toothpick inserted into the center of each cake comes out clean, 30–35 minutes. Transfer the cakes to wire racks and let cool in the pans for 20 minutes. Then invert onto plates, lift off the pans, and invert again onto the racks. Let cool completely.

Make-Ahead Tip The cake layers can be baked up to 2 days in advance, well wrapped in plastic wrap, and stored at room temperature.

Makes two 8- or 9-inch (20- or 23-cm) cake layers

All-purpose (plain) flour 2¼ cups (11½ oz/360 g)

Baking powder 1 tablespoon

Salt ¼ teaspoon

Unsalted butter ¾ cup (6 oz/185 g), at room temperature

Sugar 1¾ cups (14 oz/440 g)

Vanilla extract (essence) 1 teaspoon

Lemon extract (essence) 1 teaspoon

Lemon zest 1 tablespoon, finely grated

Large eggs 3, at room temperature

Whole milk 1⅓ cups (11 fl oz/340 ml), at room temperature

Vanilla Frosting

**Makes about 2¼ cups
(18 fl oz/560 ml)**

Unsalted butter ¾ cup (6 oz/185 g),
at room temperature

Confectioners' (icing) sugar 3¼ cups
(13 oz/410 g)

Heavy (double) cream 2 tablespoons

Vanilla extract (essence) 2 teaspoons

Salt ¼ teaspoon

● In a bowl, using an electric mixer on low speed, beat together the butter, sugar, cream, vanilla, and salt until creamy and smooth, about 3 minutes. Use the frosting right away.

Variations For lemon frosting, proceed as directed, but reduce the vanilla to 1 teaspoon and stir in 1 teaspoon lemon extract (essence) and 1 teaspoon finely grated lemon zest. To color the frosting, proceed as directed, then beat in food coloring, a drop at a time, until the desired color is achieved.

Chocolate Frosting

**Makes about 2 cups
(16 fl oz/500 ml)**

Unsweetened chocolate 4 oz
(125 g), finely chopped

Confectioners' (icing) sugar 2 cups
(8 oz/250 g)

Unsalted butter 1 cup (8 oz/250 g),
at room temperature

Vanilla extract (essence) 2 teaspoons

Heavy (double) cream ¼ cup
(2 fl oz/60 ml), at room temperature

● Place chocolate in a heatproof bowl and set over (not touching) simmering water in a saucepan. Heat, stirring occasionally, until melted and smooth, about 5 minutes. Set aside to cool for 5 minutes.

● In a large bowl, using a handheld mixer or a stand mixer fitted with the paddle attachment, beat together the sugar and butter on low speed until combined. Continue to beat on medium speed until smooth, about 1 minute longer. Beat in the vanilla, then beat in the chocolate until combined. Pour in the cream and continue to beat on medium speed until the color lightens and the mixture looks fluffy, about 1 minute. Use the frosting right away, while it is still soft and spreads easily.

Dark Chocolate Glaze

In a small, heavy saucepan over medium-low heat, combine the chocolate chips, butter, and corn syrup and stir frequently until melted and smooth, about 5 minutes.

Remove from the heat and stir in 1 to 2 teaspoons water if a thinner consistency is desired, then use immediately. Pour the glaze over the top of a cooled cake and use an icing spatula to spread it evenly over the top and onto the sides.

Suggested Use Use this glaze on single-layer cakes, where it will create a smooth and shiny finish, then top with decorations of choice, if desired.

Makes about ½ cup
(4 fl oz/125 ml)

Semisweet (plain) chocolate chips
½ cup (3 oz/90 g)

Unsalted butter 2 tablespoons

Light corn syrup 2 tablespoons

Chocolate Ganache

In a small pan over medium-low heat, combine the butter and cream and heat, stirring occasionally, just until the butter is melted and the mixture is hot. Remove from the heat and add the chocolate. Let the chocolate soften for about 30 seconds. Add the vanilla, then whisk until melted and smooth.

For use as a fudge sauce to accompany cake slices or on top of ice cream, use immediately. For use as a frosting or filling, let cool, then cover and refrigerate. Stir after 30 minutes, then continue to refrigerate, stirring every 5 minutes, until the ganache has a good spreading consistency.

Make-Ahead Tip Cover with plastic wrap and store for up to 3 days at room temperature, 10 days refrigerated, or 6 months frozen. To soften ganache after chilling, warm the bowl in a hot water bath or for a few seconds in the microwave, stirring gently until the ganache has a good spreading consistency.

Makes about 1½ cups
(12 fl oz/375 ml)

Unsalted butter 2 tablespoons

Heavy (double) cream ⅔ cup
(5 fl oz/160 ml), or as needed

Semisweet (plain) or bittersweet chocolate chips 8 oz (250 g)

Vanilla extract (essence) 1 teaspoon

Lemon Curd

**Makes 1 cup
(8 fl oz/250 ml)**

Lemon zest 1 teaspoon finely grated

Fresh lemon juice 6 tablespoons
(3 fl oz/80 ml)

Fresh orange juice 3 tablespoons

Large eggs 2, at room temperature

Sugar ⅓ cup (2½ oz/75 g)

Unsalted butter 2 tablespoons

Heavy (double) cream 2 tablespoons

In a saucepan, combine the lemon zest, lemon and orange juices, eggs, sugar, butter, and cream and whisk to blend. Place over medium heat and cook, whisking constantly, until the curd thickens and registers 165°F (74°C) on an instant-read thermometer, about 5 minutes. Watch the curd carefully and do not allow to overcook. Immediately pour into a bowl and cover with plastic wrap, pressing it directly onto the surface to prevent a skin from forming. Let cool, then refrigerate until needed. It will keep for up to 1 week.

Suggested Use Use as a filling for a vanilla (page 128) or lemon (page 131) layer cake.

Decorating Icing

**Makes about 1⅓ cups
(11 fl oz/340 ml)**

Confectioners' (icing) sugar 4 cups
(1 lb/500g)

Unsalted butter 4 tablespoons
(2 oz/60 g), melted and cooled slightly

Heavy (double) cream or milk ¼ cup
(2 fl oz/60 ml)

Vanilla extract (essence) 2 teaspoons

Food coloring (optional)

In a bowl, using an electric mixer on medium speed, beat together the confectioners' sugar, butter, cream, and vanilla. Beat with an electric mixer until blended and smooth. If necessary, add more cream to thin the icing, or more sugar to thicken it. If desired, add food coloring, tinting the whole batch a single color or separating the glaze into small bowls to make different colors.

Decorating Tip To use this glaze for decorating cookies or cake tops, spoon it into a regular or disposable pastry (piping) bag fitted with a plain tip, or into a lock-top plastic bag and snip off a corner.

Strawberry Mousse Filling

● Using a blender or food processor, purée the berries until smooth. Pour into a small bowl and stir in the sugar. Set aside.

● In a small microwave-safe bowl, sprinkle the gelatin over the water. Let stand for 2 minutes to soften, then microwave on High for 30 seconds (or stir over a bowl of hot water) to dissolve the gelatin. Do not boil. Let cool slightly, then stir into the purée.

● In a bowl, using an electric mixer on medium-high speed or a whisk, whip the cream until soft peaks form. Stir in the berry purée until blended. Refrigerate, stirring every few minutes, until the mousse begins to thicken, about 15 minutes. (Or, stir over a bowl of ice water until thickened.) Use immediately.

Suggested Use Line the bottom and sides of a deep springform pan the same diameter as the cake layers with plastic wrap. Place 1 cake layer on the bottom, spread evenly with the mousse, then top with the second cake layer. Refrigerate until firm, about 1 hour. Carefully remove the pan sides and the plastic wrap and frost the cake as desired.

Whipped Cream

● In a bowl, combine the cream, sugar, and vanilla. Using an electric mixer on medium-high speed or a whisk, whip until soft peaks form. Use at once, or cover and refrigerate for up to 24 hours. Whisk lightly before serving.

Lemon Variation Mix equal parts of Lemon Curd (opposite) and whipped cream for a light, lemony cake filling or topping.

**Makes about 1½ cups
(12 fl oz/375 ml)**

Fresh or thawed frozen sliced strawberries 1 cup (4 oz/125 g)

Sugar 2 tablespoons

Powdered gelatin 2 teaspoons

Water ¼ cup (2 fl oz/60 ml)

Cold heavy (double) cream 1 cup (8 fl oz/250 ml)

**Makes about 2 cups
(16 fl oz/500 ml)**

Cold heavy (double) cream 1 cup (8 fl oz/250 ml)

Sugar 1½ tablespoons

Vanilla extract (essence) ½ teaspoon

Vanilla Ice Cream

Cold heavy (double) cream 2 cups
(16 fl oz/500 ml)

Cold whole milk 1 cup (8 fl oz/250 ml)

Sugar, preferably superfine (caster)
¾ cup (6 oz/185 g)

Vanilla extract (essence) 1 tablespoon

● In a large bowl, whisk together the cream and milk. Add the sugar and whisk until completely dissolved, 3–4 minutes. Stir in the vanilla. Cover and refrigerate for 3 hours or up to 24 hours.

● Pour the cream mixture into an ice cream maker and freeze according to the manufacturer's instructions. Transfer to a freezer-safe container and freeze until firm, at least 3 hours or up to 3 days, before serving.

Mint Chip Variation Substitute 1½ teaspoons peppermint extract (essence) for the vanilla. Add ¾ cup (4½ oz/140 g) semisweet (plain) chocolate chips to the ice cream maker during the last 5 minutes of freezing time.

Cookie Dough Variation Add ¾ cup (4½ oz/140 g) store-bought chocolate chip cookie dough in spoon-sized lumps to the ice cream maker during the last 5 minutes of freezing time.

Cookies & Cream Variation Add ¾ cup (4½ oz/140 g) coarsely chopped Oreo cookies, chocolate chip cookies, or other favorite cookies to the ice cream maker during the last 5 minutes of freezing time.

Strawberry Variation Reduce the vanilla to 1 teaspoon. Add 2 cups (8 oz/250 g) strawberries, hulled and coarsely chopped, to the ice cream maker during the last 1 minute of freezing time.

Caramel Swirl Variation When transferring the ice cream from the ice cream maker to the freezer container, layer the ice cream in the container with about 1 cup (8 fl oz/250 ml) cooled Quick Caramel Sauce (page 138), alternating 4 equal layers of ice cream with 4 equal layers of sauce.

Chocolate Ice Cream

In a heavy 2-qt (2-l) saucepan over medium heat, combine the milk and 1 cup (8 fl oz/250 ml) of the cream and heat until small bubbles appear around the edges of the pan, about 5 minutes. Remove from the heat.

Put the chocolate in a heatproof bowl. Pour the hot milk mixture over the chocolate. Let stand until melted, about 3 minutes, then stir until smooth.

Meanwhile, in a separate bowl, combine the egg yolks, sugar, salt, and the remaining ½ cup (4 fl oz/125 ml) cream. Whisk until smooth and the sugar begins to dissolve.

Gradually whisk about ½ cup (4 fl oz/125 ml) of the warm milk mixture into the egg mixture until smooth. Pour the egg mixture into the saucepan and stir in the remaining milk mixture. Cook over medium heat, stirring constantly with a wooden spoon and maintaining a low simmer, until the custard is thick enough to coat the back of the spoon and leaves a clear trail when a finger is drawn through it, 4–6 minutes. Do not boil. Strain through a fine-mesh sieve into a clean bowl. Add the vanilla and stir to combine.

Place the bowl in a large bowl partially filled with ice cubes and water. Stir occasionally until cool, then cover with plastic wrap, pressing it directly onto the surface to prevent a skin from forming. Refrigerate until chilled, at least 3 hours or up to 24 hours.

Pour the custard into an ice cream maker and freeze according to the manufacturer's instructions. Transfer to a freezer-safe container and freeze until firm, at least 3 hours or up to 3 days, before serving.

Rocky Road Variation Add ¼ cup (1 oz/30 g) coarsely chopped walnuts and ¼ cup (½ oz/15 g) miniature marshmallows to the ice cream maker during the last 5 minutes of freezing time.

Chocolate Marble Fudge Variation When transferring the ice cream from the ice cream maker to the freezer container, layer the ice cream with about 1 cup (8 fl oz/250 ml) cooled Chocolate Fudge Sauce (page 138), alternating 4 equal layers of ice cream with 4 equal layers of sauce.

Makes about 1 qt (1 l)

Whole milk 1½ cups (12 fl oz/375 ml)

Heavy (double) cream 1½ cups (12 fl oz/375 ml)

Semisweet (plain) chocolate 6 oz (185 g), coarsely chopped

Large egg yolks 4, at room temperature

Sugar ½ cup (4 oz/125 g)

Salt pinch

Vanilla extract (essence) 1 teaspoon

Chocolate Fudge Sauce

**Makes about 1 cup
(8 fl oz/250 ml)**

Heavy (double) cream ⅔ cup
(5 fl oz/160 ml)

Light corn syrup ½ cup (5 oz/155 g)

Light brown sugar 2 tablespoons
firmly packed

Semisweet (plain) chocolate, 5 oz
(155 g), coarsely chopped

Salt pinch

Vanilla extract (essence) 1 teaspoon

In a heavy saucepan over medium-low heat, combine the cream, corn syrup, and brown sugar. Bring to a boil, stirring occasionally until the sugar dissolves, about 5 minutes. In a bowl, combine the chocolate and salt. Pour the hot cream mixture over the chocolate and stir until melted and smooth. Add the vanilla and stir to combine. Use immediately, or let cool, cover, and refrigerate for up to 1 week. Reheat or use at room temperature or chilled.

Suggested Uses Spoon hot or room-temperature sauce over cake or ice cream, or layer with freshly made Chocolate Ice Cream (page 137) to create a marbled effect.

Quick Caramel Sauce

**Makes about 1⅓ cups
(11 fl oz/340 ml)**

Caramels 1 bag (14 oz/440 g)

Evaporated milk ¼ cup (2 fl oz/60 ml)

Unsalted butter 2 tablespoons

In a small saucepan over medium heat, combine the caramels and milk. Heat, stirring often, until melted and smooth, about 5 minutes. Stir in the butter until combined. Use immediately, or let cool, cover, and refrigerate for up to 1 week. Reheat or use at room temperature or chilled.

Suggested Uses Spoon hot or room-temperature sauce over cake or ice cream, or layer with freshly made Vanilla Ice Cream (page 136) to create a swirled effect.

This sweet, syrupy sauce can be served over ice cream or pooled under a slice of cake. It brings a touch of bright color and an intense strawberry flavor to every serving.

Strawberry Sauce

- Put the strawberries in a sieve set over a bowl. Let thaw at room temperature until the juices are liquid but the berries are still partially frozen. Reserve ½ cup (4 fl oz/125 ml) of the juice. Transfer the berries to another bowl and set aside.

- Put the arrowroot in a small cup and slowly stir in about 1 tablespoon of the strawberry juice until smooth. Pour the remaining juice into a small saucepan over medium heat and stir in the arrowroot mixture. Continue to stir until the mixture comes to a boil, then immediately remove from the heat. Pour the syrup over the berries and stir to combine. Transfer the mixture to a blender or a food processor and pulse to purée. Strain through a fine-mesh sieve into a bowl or serving pitcher. Cover and refrigerate until chilled, at least 2 hours or up to 2 days, before serving.

Makes about 1 cup
(8 fl oz/250 ml)

Sweetened frozen strawberries
1 bag (10 oz/315 g)

Arrowroot or cornstarch 2 teaspoons

This basic, versatile butter-rich dough makes a plain cookie that's ideal for decorating (page 21). You can make the dough up to 3 days before baking; wrap it in plastic wrap and refrigerate.

Makes about 3 dozen
2-inch (5-cm) cookies

All-purpose (plain) flour 1½ cups
(7½ oz/235 g)

Baking powder 1 teaspoon

Salt ¼ teaspoon

Unsalted butter ½ cup (4 oz/125 g),
at room temperature

Sugar ¾ cup (6 oz/185 g)

Large egg 1

Vanilla extract (essence) 1½ teaspoons

Sugar Cookies

● In a bowl, stir together the flour, baking powder, and salt. Set aside.

● In a large bowl, using a handheld mixer or a stand mixer fitted with the paddle attachment, beat together the butter and sugar on medium-high speed until combined. Add the egg and vanilla and beat until light and creamy, 2–3 minutes. With the mixer on low speed, gradually beat in the flour mixture just until blended.

● Divide the dough in half, and wrap each half in plastic wrap, pressing the dough into a flat disk. Refrigerate until firm, about 1 hour.

● Preheat the oven to 350°F (180°C). Unwrap one-half of the dough and set on a lightly floured work surface. Using a lightly floured rolling pin, roll out the dough into a round ⅛ inch (3 mm) thick, lifting the dough occasionally and lightly sprinkling it and the surface with flour as needed to prevent sticking. Using cookie cutters, cut out as many shapes as possible and space each cookie about ½ inch (12 mm) apart on an ungreased baking sheet. Gather up the scraps, press into a flat disk, rewrap, and return to the refrigerator.

● Bake until lightly golden, 10–12 minutes. Meanwhile, roll out the remaining half of the dough, cut out shapes, and place on a second baking sheet. Gather up the scraps and refrigerate.

● When the first batch of cookies is done, remove it from the oven and slip in the second batch. Let the first batch cool briefly on the pan, and then transfer the cookies to wire racks and let cool completely. Cool the second batch the same way, and then shape and bake the dough scraps to make more cookies. The cookies will keep in an airtight container for up to 3 days.

Easy for kids to work with, this dough holds together well and makes a slightly cakey cookie. Enjoy them plain, or decorate with icing (page 134) and customize with toppings that fit your party theme.

Gingerbread Cookies

In a bowl, mix the flour, baking powder, ginger, cinnamon, nutmeg, and salt. Set aside.

In a large bowl, using a handheld mixer or a stand mixer fitted with the paddle attachment, beat together the butter, brown sugar, and vanilla on medium speed until creamy, about 3 minutes. Scrape down the sides of the bowl with a rubber spatula. Add the egg and molasses and beat on medium speed until blended. With the mixer on low speed, gradually beat in the flour mixture just until incorporated.

Press the dough together into a mound. Divide in half and wrap each half in plastic wrap, pressing the dough into flat disks. Refrigerate for at least 1 hour or up to 2 days.

Preheat the oven to 350°F (180°C). Lightly butter 2 baking sheets. Unwrap one half of the dough and set on a lightly floured work surface. Roll out the dough into a round about ¼ inch (6 mm) thick, lifting the dough occasionally and lightly sprinkling the work surface with flour as needed to prevent sticking. Using cookie cutters, cut out as many shapes as possible and space them about 1 inch (2.5 cm) apart on the prepared baking sheets. Gather up the scraps, press into a flat disk, rewrap, and return to the refrigerator.

Bake until the edges are lightly browned, 10–12 minutes. Meanwhile, roll out the remaining half of the dough, cut out shapes, and place on a second baking sheet. Gather up the scraps and refrigerate.

When the first batch of cookies is done, remove it from the oven and slip in the second batch. Let the first batch cool briefly on the pan, and then transfer the cookies to wire racks and let cool completely. Cool the second batch the same way, and then shape and bake the dough scraps to make more cookies. The cookies will keep in an airtight container for up to 3 days.

Makes about 2 dozen 3-inch (7.6-cm) cookies

All-purpose (plain) flour 2¾ cups (13½ oz/425 g)

Baking powder 2½ teaspoons

Ground ginger 1 tablespoon

Ground cinnamon, 1½ teaspoons

Ground nutmeg ½ teaspoon

Salt ¼ teaspoon

Unsalted butter ½ cup (4 oz/125 g), at room temperature

Light brown sugar ⅔ cup (5 oz/155 g) firmly packed

Vanilla extract (essence) 1 teaspoon

Large egg 1

Dark molasses ⅓ cup (4 oz/125 g)

Index

A

Apples, Caramel, 93

B

Backyard parties, 52–66
  activities, 61, 63
  decorations, 56, 57, 58
  favors, 56, 58
  food ideas, 56, 57, 58
  invitations, 56
  planning, 60
  recipes, 64–66
Bananas
  Fruit Smoothies, 79
  Lava Flows, 79
Beverages
  Blood-Red Punch, 93
  Fresh-Squeezed Lemonade, 48
  Fruit Smoothies, 79
  Hot Spiced Cider, 123
  Lava Flows, 79
  Pink Lemonade, 48
  Snugglers, 123
Birthday parties, 9–21
  activities, 11
  decorations, 9
  favors, 10, 21
  food ideas, 13–21
  planning, 11
  recipes, 128–41
  themes, 10
Blood-Red Punch, 93
Bread, Pumpkin, 95
Butters, Flavored, 65

C

Cakes
  Chocolate Cake, 129
  decorating, 13, 14, 16, 17, 21
  Lemon Cake, 131
  Marble Cake, 130
  themed, 16
  types of, 13
  Vanilla Cake, 128

Caramel
  Caramel Apples, 93
  Caramel Swirl Ice Cream, 136
  Quick Caramel Sauce, 138
Carrot Cupcakes, Garden-Top, 50
Cheese
  Cheese Fondue, 124
  Cream Cheese Frosting, 50
Chex Mix, 64
Chicken Kebabs, Hawaiian, 80
Chocolate
  Chocolate Cake, 129
  Chocolate Cupcakes, 35
  Chocolate-Dipped Caramel Apples, 93
  Chocolate Fondue, 125
  Chocolate Frosting, 132
  Chocolate Fudge Sauce, 138
  Chocolate Ganache, 133
  Chocolate Ice Cream, 137
  Chocolate Marble Fudge Ice Cream, 137
  Cookie Dough Ice Cream, 136
  Cookies and Cream Ice Cream, 136
  Dark Chocolate Glaze, 133
  "Dirty" Popcorn Balls, 94
  Easter Egg Lollipops, 47, 49
  Marble Cake, 130
  Marble Cupcakes, 34
  Mint Chip Ice Cream, 136
  Rocky Road Ice Cream, 137
  S'mores, 63, 66
  Snugglers, 123
Cider, Hot Spiced, 123
Cinnamon Spice Butter, 65
Cookie parties, 20
Cookies
  as cake decorations, 21
  as party treats, 21
  Cookie Dough Ice Cream, 136
  Cookies and Cream Ice Cream, 136
  Gingerbread Cookies, 141
  ideas for, 20
  Sugar Cookies, 140
Corn
  Corn on the Cobettes, 65
  "Dirty" Popcorn Balls, 94
Cream, Whipped, 135
Cream Cheese Frosting, 50

Cupcake parties, 22–35
  activities, 31, 33
  decorations, 26, 27, 28
  favors, 26, 28
  food ideas, 26, 27, 28
  invitations, 26
  planning, 30
  recipes, 34–35
Cupcakes
  Chocolate Cupcakes, 35
  decorating, 33
  Garden-Top Carrot Cupcakes, 50
  Marble Cupcakes, 34
  Vanilla Cupcakes, 34

D

Decorating Icing, 134
Decorations. *See individual parties*
"Dirty" Popcorn Balls, 94
Dressing, Creamy Garlic, 110

E

Easter Egg Lollipops, 47, 49
Easter parties, 36–50
  activities, 45
  decorations, 40, 41, 43
  favors, 40
  food ideas, 40, 41, 43
  invitations, 40
  planning, 44
  recipes, 48–50

F

Favors. *See individual parties*
Fondant, 17
Fondue
  Cheese Fondue, 124
  Chocolate Fondue, 125
Frostings, icings, and glazes
  Chocolate Frosting, 132
  Chocolate Ganache, 133
  Cream Cheese Frosting, 50
  Dark Chocolate Glaze, 133
  Decorating Icing, 134
  Vanilla Frosting, 132
Fruit Smoothies, 79

G

Ganache, Chocolate, 133
Garden-Top Carrot Cupcakes, 50
Garlic
    Creamy Garlic Dressing, 110
    Roasted Garlic Butter, 65
Gingerbread Cookies, 141
Glazes. *See Frostings, icings, and glazes*
Graham crackers
    S'mores, 63, 66

H

Halloween parties, 82–95
    activities, 91
    decorations, 86, 87
    favors, 86, 87
    food ideas, 86, 88
    invitations, 86, 87
    planning, 90
    recipes, 93–95
Hawaiian Chicken Kebabs, 80

I

Ice cream
    cake with, 18
    Caramel Swirl Ice Cream, 136
    Chocolate Ice Cream, 137
    Chocolate Marble Fudge Ice Cream, 137
    Cookie Dough Ice Cream, 136
    Cookies and Cream Ice Cream, 136
    Mint Chip Ice Cream, 136
    Rocky Road Ice Cream, 137
    sandwiches, 18
    sodas, 18
    Strawberry Ice Cream, 136
    sundae parties, 19
    Vanilla Ice Cream, 136
Ice Cubes, Scary, 93
Icings. *See Frostings, icings, and glazes*
Invitations. *See individual parties*

K & L

Kebabs, Hawaiian Chicken, 80
Lava Flows, 79
Lemons
    Fresh-Squeezed Lemonade, 48
    Lemon Cake, 131

Lemon Curd, 134
    Pink Lemonade, 48
Lollipops, Easter Egg, 47, 49

M

Mangoes
    Fruit Smoothies, 79
    Mango Dipping Sauce, 80
Maple Butter, 65
Marble Cake, 130
Marble Cupcakes, 34
Marshmallows
    "Dirty" Popcorn Balls, 94
    Rocky Road Ice Cream, 137
    S'mores, 63, 66
Melon Ball Salad, 48
Mint Chip Ice Cream, 136

P & R

Pecan Butter, 65
Pink Lemonade, 48
Pizza parties, 96–110
    activities, 102, 105
    decorations, 100, 101
    favors, 100, 101
    food ideas, 100, 101
    invitations, 100
    planning, 104
    recipes, 108–10
Pizzas
    making, 107
    Pizza Dough, 108
Popcorn Balls, "Dirty," 94
Pumpkin Bread, 95
Punch, Blood-Red, 93
Raspberries
    Blood-Red Punch, 93
Rocky Road Ice Cream, 137

S

Salads
    Chopped Green Salad, 110
    Melon Ball Salad, 48
Sauces
    Chocolate Fudge Sauce, 138
    Chocolate Ganache, 133
    Mango Dipping Sauce, 80

Quick Caramel Sauce, 138
    Quick Tomato Sauce, 109
    Strawberry Sauce, 139
Sausages, Fire-Roasted, on Sticks, 66
Scary Ice Cubes, 93
Smoothies, Fruit, 79
S'mores, 63, 66
Snugglers, 123
Strawberries
    Blood-Red Punch, 93
    Lava Flows, 79
    Strawberry Ice Cream, 136
    Strawberry Mousse Filling, 135
    Strawberry Sauce, 139
Sugar Cookies, 140
Sundae parties, 19

T

Tiki parties, 68–80
    activities, 73, 77
    decorations, 72, 73, 74
    favors, 73
    food ideas, 72, 73, 74
    invitations, 72
    planning, 76
    recipes, 79–80
Tomato Sauce, Quick, 109

V

Vanilla
    Vanilla Cake, 128
    Vanilla Cupcakes, 34
    Vanilla Frosting, 132
    Vanilla Ice Cream, 136

W

Whipped Cream, 135
White chocolate
    Easter Egg Lollipops, 47, 49
Winter parties, 112–25
    activities, 121
    decorations, 116, 117, 118
    favors, 116
    food ideas, 116, 117, 118
    invitations, 116
    planning, 120
    recipes, 123–25

Oxmoor
House.

OXMOOR HOUSE

Oxmoor House books are distributed by Sunset Books
80 Willow Road, Menlo Park, CA 94025
Telephone: 650 324 1532
VP and Associate Publisher Jim Childs
Director of Sales Brad Moses
Oxmoor House and Sunset Books are divisions
of Southern Progress Corporation

WILLIAMS-SONOMA, INC.
Founder & Vice-Chairman Chuck Williams

WILLIAMS-SONOMA *KIDS PARTIES*
Conceived and produced by Weldon Owen Inc.
415 Jackson Street, San Francisco, CA 94111
Telephone: 415 291 0100 Fax: 415 291 8841

In Collaboration with Williams-Sonoma, Inc.
3250 Van Ness Avenue, San Francisco, CA 94109

A WELDON OWEN PRODUCTION
Copyright © 2007 Weldon Owen Inc. and Williams-Sonoma, Inc.
All rights reserved, including the right of reproduction
in whole or in part in any form.

First printed in 2007
Printed in China

Printed by SNP-Leefung
10 9 8 7 6 5 4 3 2
Library of Congress Cataloging-in-Publication Data is available.

ISBN-13: 978-0-8487-3240-0
ISBN-10: 0-8487-3240-5

WELDON OWEN INC.

CEO, Weldon Owen Group John Owen
CEO and President, Weldon Owen Inc. Terry Newell
CFO, Weldon Owen Group Simon Fraser
VP, Sales and New Business Development Amy Kaneko
VP, International Sales Stuart Laurence
VP and Creative Director Gaye Allen
VP and Publisher Hannah Rahill

Associate Publisher Amy Marr
Senior Art Director Emma Boys
Designer Diana Heom
Production Director Chris Hemesath
Production Manager Michelle Duggan
Color Manager Teri Bell
Photo Manager Meghan Hildebrand

Photo Assistants Marcus Guillard, Brian Slaughter
Digital Technician David Turek
Assistant Food Stylist Jeffrey Larson
Assistant Prop Stylists Stephanie Corbridge, Taylor McCarthy

Additional Photography Bill Bettencourt (pages 43 and 51, upper left)

ACKNOWLEDGMENTS
Weldon Owen wishes to thank the following individuals for their kind assistance:
Ken DellaPenta, Lesli Neilson, Kathryn Shedrick, Sharon Silva, and Kate Washington.
Homeowners Matt and Shannon Violante, Alexis Glavin, and Greg and Susan Genovese.
Models Austin Andriatico, Gage Atwood, Isabella Barbero, Malia Berry, Connor Bock,
Katie Calderon, Lucia and Thomas Chuaqui-Schmida, Abraham Clay, Hanna and Lilli
Corny, Isabelle Eggert, Gemma Fa-Kaji, Gregory Genovese, Molly Gibbons, Holly Hogan,
Esme Judd-Donaldson, Grant Keffeler, Gabriel and Jeremy Leary, Madeleine and Sophia
Lincoln, Connor and Reilly McLoy, Alyssa Oberhauser, Jacob and Julia Prager, Eli Svoboda,
Tatum Quon, Giordana Simurdiak, Isaiah Sterling, Claire Tauber, Piper Todd, Devon Violante,
Bayard and Duncan Walsh, Alexandra and Samantha Webber, and Dayton White.